Different values shape the world we live in and we are, consequently, pulled in different directions. It is difficult to always remember our value as beloved sons and daughters of God. We jump on the treadmill of achievement and success from the moment we learn to walk and never come off until we chaperoned to the cemetery. Living in Dominion, using scriptural insights and psychological findings, challenges us to become aware of our fundamental identity. This identity gives us an edge in a world gone hire wire.

Fr. Joseph Salihu, Ph.D.

In this thoughtful, well written book, Father Emmanuel Mbah, explores the many ways we, as Christian people, share in the reign of God. The author has come to a powerful understanding that along with this gift of "dominion" comes great responsibility to enact this wonderful truth in all aspects of our lives. Father Emmanuel shows us the way to "everyday holiness" through his reflections on such practicalities as: prayer, hard work, generosity, physical exercise, retreat & vacation etc. As a Christian pilgrim searching for a path, this book will empower you for the journey.

Helen Mourre, parishioner at St. Theresa' Catholic Church, Rosetown, Saskatchewan, Canada, author of *To Everything A Season.*

This book simply captures the very essence of the *'dominion mandate'* given by God, the great architect to mankind.

It states that man is a product of an all wise Creator who brought us into the world for successful living - *living in purpose for fruitfulness.*

It offers points of reflection from a wide variety of sources to readers not to drift upon the stormy sea of life, but to live in dominion, and so find health, wealth and happiness.

The object of the book is a purpose driven life for victorious living according to the dominion mandate.

So, it comes to us as an extraordinary source of inspiration and encouragement for a victorious living in Christ.

Very Revd Fr Michael Adefemi Adegbola
Vicar General, Catholic Diocese of Kano, Nigeria.

LIVING IN DOMINION

A BIO-PSYCHO-SOCIAL-SPIRITUAL LIFE

Fr Emmanuel Mbah

◆ FriesenPress

Suite 300 - 990 Fort St
Victoria, BC, V8V 3K2
Canada

www.friesenpress.com

ISBN
978-1-5255-1415-9 (Hardcover)
978-1-5255-1416-6 (Paperback)
978-1-5255-1417-3 (eBook)

1. RELIGION, SPIRITUALITY

Distributed to the trade by The Ingram Book Company

Table of Contents

Nihil obstat

- Fr. Joseph Salihu, Ph.D.

Imprimatur

Most Rev. Dr John N. Niyiring, OSA
Bishop of Kano Diocese.

Dedication

To Ken (Margaret) Ogle whose life has been a miracle, and his resilience has always inspired me. Ken was diagnosed of Cancer 62 in 2009, and was given 6 to 12 months to live by the doctors. But after 8 years, Ken is still living to the amazement of everyone especially his doctor. According to Ken, "I have made it thus far, because of 4 Fs: Faith, Family, Friends and Fun." And his doctor added, "Plus a good physician". The 4 Fs' principle is part of the inspiration for this book.

Also to all the parishioners of St Theresa's Rosetown, St Theresa's Beechy and Immaculate Heart of Mary Elrose. Their faith and pleasant demeanour in the face of life's challenges have also inspired me and helped me grow.

Acknowledgement

Thank you to everyone who has contributed to the realisation of this book. Worthy of note are Bishop John N. Niyiring, OSA and Archbishop Donald Bolen, for providing me a place for ministry. Most of the reflections in this book are the fruits of my experience in ministry. My special gratitude and indebtedness to Fr Joseph Salihu, PhD and Virginia Mireau who took their time to edit this work. Likewise, to Fr Peter Ebidero for the special insights he brought to the work and taking his time to write the forward. Thank you to my colleagues during the Clinical and Pastoral Education (CPE), especially Fr Emmanuel Olusola, PhD, and the teaching supervisor – Brian Walton. Some of the experiences we shared in class informed part of this book.

A tribute of gratitude to Helen Mourre for the professional advice she offered, and her endorsement of the book. Special thanks to Fr Patrick Ampani, Kim Askin, Agatha Kalu, Fr Isaac Agu and Fr Charles Achi for always believing in me and encouraging me to be strong and do more. Thank you too to Fr Fredrick Aka, MSP and Fr Peter Nnanga, MSP, for their prayerful support.

I thank my mother – Felicia Mbah, and my siblings: I will always appreciate the love we share. This love has inspired me in so many ways. Thanks to "Papa" (my father – Lawrence Mbah), for laying the foundation. May you continue to rest in the bosom of Abraham.

Fr Emmanuel Ndubuisi Mbah.

Forward

Success connotes living in dominion, every man and woman walking on God's green earth desires dominion in all areas of life. Even nations work hard in ensuring their economic, social and military dominion remain the best among their equals. As I see it, living in dominion mind-set is strategic for individual and national advancement.

Reading through this book, I got immersed into numerous bible truths which every Christian must live by in order to live in DOMINION in every area of life. One ringing truth in this book as written by Fr. Emmanuel is... "*Living in dominion is putting everything in the right perspective, and in the right proportion, paying the right attention to every aspect of your existence without neglecting any aspect. It means ensuring your biological (physical) and psychological well-being, while*

maintaining a spiritual and social balance in the society."
I couldn't agree more.

That said, knowing who you are is key element in your quest for living in dominion in all areas of your life. This, Fr. Emmanuel presented in graphic and succinct way. According to him you cannot operate God's type of reasoning and be a victim of self-depreciation. He made it clear that when you understand the depth and power that comes with the statement "...have dominion" as commanded by God, you will never have problem overcoming life's numerous challenges.

Moving further, the book contains doses of bible nuggets on dealing with poor self-worth and I highly recommend you reading through in order to understand and overcome the dangers that comes with it.

On a final note, principle add value to you, it makes you resilient and grounded when the storms of life roar. Living life without the right principles will obviously lead towards an irredeemable crash. As you read this book, you will encounter biblical and time tested principles, when applied will usher you into a world of stability, empowerment and living in complete dominion.

Fr Peter Ebidero

Part 1
The Nature and Meaning of Dominion

The first part of this book contains a detailed explanation of what living in dominion entails, as God's original plan for his children, means for us as Christians: How it was lost in Adam, and found in Christ.

Chapter 1
Living in Dominion

When we talk about living in dominion, the immediate thought that comes to mind is the act of domination, that is, to dominate or to take over. This, at times, can be perceived negatively. For example, it is not a compliment when friends speak about you as being domineering - one who will always like to dominate discussions. In other words, you hardly listen to others. You are "Mr. Know It All", and every other person should listen while you speak. This kind of domination leaves one basking in the air of pride and self-centredness. And before long, people will want to avoid such a person.

The same is applicable to those who will want to acquire or take over people's property, possessions and belongings at all cost, because they want to dominate. This is not what living in dominion means in the actual sense of the word. Moreover, the tenth commandment of God clearly states: "You shall not covet your neighbour's house; you shall not covet your neighbour's wife, or his manservant, or his maidservant, or his ox, or his donkey, or anything that is your neighbour's" (Exodus 20:17). So, besides the fact that this commandment forbids avarice, arising from a passion for riches and their attendant power, it also forbids the desire to commit injustice by harming our neighbour in his or her temporal good (CCC #2536).

Genesis 1:27-28 states: "So God created man in his own image, in the image of God he created him; male and female he created them. And God blessed them, and God said to them, "Be fruitful and multiply; and fill the earth and subdue it; and have **dominion** over the fish of the sea and over the birds of the air and over every living thing that moves upon the earth." This is a mandate that God gave to humanity to share in His reign. It is, however, not about intimidating a neighbour and taking over his or her acquisitions with force. It is a spiritual dominion in which one is invited to share in the reign of God.

To "reign over" something is to have absolute authority and control over it. God has ultimate rule over the earth and exercises his authority with loving care.

When God delegated some of his authority to the human race, he expected us to take responsibility for the environment and the other creatures that share our planet. This responsibility also includes self-care. As such, living in dominion is a call to all-around fitness - living in a way that keeps you physically, psychologically, socially and spiritually fit. Preventing any health issues resulting from carelessness or negligence towards your physical well-being, or towards your environment and your spiritual life (like lack of exercise and eating of all the wrong food, too much consumption of alcohol, smoking and other habits that are detrimental to health). We must not be careless and wasteful as we fulfil this charge.

God was purposeful, and took his time when he made this earth; and was even more purposeful, taking extra time in creating us. As such, we must not be careless about how we take care of God's creatures – the earth and ourselves.

Living in dominion is putting everything in the right perspective, and in the right proportion, paying the right attention to every aspect of your existence without neglecting any aspect. It means ensuring your biological (physical) and psychological well-being, while maintaining a spiritual and social balance in the society. The problem so many are having today is that they focus on one aspect of life to the detriment of the others. Some do this out of ignorance because they think that these different aspects of human existence are exclusive and cannot go together. Or they feel that trying to keep up with all of them is overwhelming. The purpose of this write-up is to clarify the significance of each aspect of life and possibility of paying attention to all of them, since that is God's design for our lives.

Chapter 2
The Dominion of Jesus

To live in dominion is God's original plan for all humanity, but this plan was thwarted through the fall of our first parents – Adam and Eve. In the second account of creation, "The Lord God planted a garden in Eden, in the east; and there he put the man whom he had formed" (Genesis 2:8). The reason why God brought man into this beautiful garden was for man to take charge and care for it – "The Lord God took man and put him in the garden of Eden to till it and to keep it" (Genesis 2:15). However, he left man an instruction: "You may freely eat of every tree of the garden; but of the tree of the knowledge of good and evil you shall not eat, for in the day that you eat of it you shall die" (Genesis 2:17). God demanded obedience from humanity through our first parents. (We shall see why God constantly demands obedience from us in Chapter 5).

Afterwards, God also created woman as a companion for man (Genesis 2:21-23). Both were then put in the garden; to live in dominion and enjoy an everlasting friendship with God. But they lost this friendship and privilege as a result of the sin of disobedience (Genesis 3:1-19). They chose to listen to the serpent instead of keeping to God's instruction. God, being holy, he responded in a way that is consistent with his perfect moral nature. He could not allow sin to go unchecked. Hence, they were sent out of the garden as a consequence for their sin. Disobedience is sin, and it breaks our fellowship with God.

Due to the disobedience of Adam and Eve, every human being ever born, with the exception of Jesus Christ and his mother Mary (see Catholic teaching on the Immaculate Conception of the Blessed Virgin Mary), has inherited the sinful nature of Adam and Eve (Romans 5:12-21). Through Adam we lost friendship with God, we lost control over self and other created things, and became subjected to the oppression and manipulation of Satan. Sin, shame and death came into the world through them. We lost our spiritual sight; the ability to see things for what they really are; and our physical grip over created things; the ability to be fully in-charge. Humanity lost its power and became powerless and weak; fill with limitations and shortcomings.

But, fortunately, God is also merciful and forgiving in his love. When we disobey, God is willing to forgive us and to restore our relationship with him. It is to repair this original fault of Adam and Eve that God came up with another plan that found its fulfilment in Christ. As a revelation of this plan, God said to the Serpent, "I will put enmity between you and the woman, and between your seed and her seed; he shall bruise your head, and you shall bruise his heel" (Genesis 3:15). Some biblical commentaries, reflecting on this verse state, that the phrase, "…you will bruise his heel" refers to Satan's repeated attempts to defeat Christ during his life on earth; while, "he shall bruise your head" foreshadows Satan's defeat when Christ rose from the dead. A bruise on the heel is not as deadly as a bruise on the head. But of great significance is that at this point God was revealing his plan to defeat Satan and offer salvation to the world through his Son, Jesus Christ.

So, the dominion of Jesus Christ is the restoration of all that we lost through Adam and Eve. Humanity lost its power in Adam and Eve, and found it in Jesus Christ. In the course of his ministry, Jesus will say, "All authority in heaven and on earth has been given to me" (Matthew 28:18).

The dominion of Jesus flows from his union with the Father. Before he came to be born, his birth was prophesied: "For to us a child is born, to us a son is given; and the government will be upon his shoulder, and his name will be called "wonderful Counsellor, Mighty God, Everlasting Father, Prince of Peace." Of the increase of his government and of peace there will be no end, upon the throne of David, and over his kingdom, to establish it, and to uphold it with justice and with righteousness from this time forth and for evermore. The zeal of the Lord of hosts will do this" (Isaiah 9:6-7). God prepared for the coming of His only begotten Son into the world. In another prophesy, the scripture has it: "And to him was given dominion and glory and kingdom, that all peoples, nations, and languages should serve him; his dominion is an everlasting dominion, which shall not pass away, and his kingdom one that shall not be destroyed" (Daniel 7:14).

The dominion of Jesus Christ is a spiritual dominion, and he shares the same substance with the Father: "I and the Father are one" (John 10:30). "I can do nothing of my own authority; as I hear, I judge; and my judgment is just, because I seek not my own will but the will of him who sent me" (John 5:30). The dominion of Jesus Christ is encapsulated in obedience to the Father. Jesus was tempted in the same way as Adam and Eve. In Matthew's gospel, after Jesus had been baptized by John, "Jesus was led up by the spirit into the wilderness to be tempted by the devil. And he fasted forty days and forty nights, and afterward he was hungry. But Jesus did not give in to any of the lures of the devil. Hence, the writer to the Hebrews will say, "For we have not a high priest who is unable to sympathize with our weaknesses, but one who in every respect has been tempted as we are, yet without sinning" (4:15). Jesus chose the way of obedience to the Father, and was able to overcome the temptations of the devil.

The dominion of Jesus Christ also has a bio-psycho-social dimensions. This is evident from the way he lived. In the course of his ministry, he worked many signs that show his power over nature: He healed the sick (both physical, spiritual and mental illness), raised the dead, rested when he felt exhausted, retreated in prayers to the Father, fed the hungry, visited the sick and socialized. At the end of the day, the scripture said, that the people were astonished beyond measure saying, "He has done all thing well" (Mark 7:37). Though, not "well enough" to save him from being unjustly condemned to death. He remained obedient to God even to the point of death (Philippians 2:8).

The apogee of Jesus' dominion is his power over death, as seen in the passion narrative. During his earthly ministry, some of the Scribes and Pharisees, together with the partisans of Herod connived to kill him. The charges they brought against him were expelling demons, forgiving sins, healing on the Sabbath day, familiarity with tax collectors and public sinners. But Jesus was not afraid to die because he knew he has dominion over death.

Even before his death while in Jerusalem, he found in the temple those who were selling oxen and sheep and pigeons, and the money changers at their business. He couldn't stand the sight of his Father's house being turned into the den of robbers, "And making a whip of cords, he drove them all, with the sheep and oxen, out of the temple; and he poured out the coins of the money-changers and overturned their tables. And he told those who sold the pigeons, "Take these things away; you shall not make my Father's house a house of trade." It was at this point, that the disciples remembered the writings of the Old Testament that states:

"Zeal for your house will consume me" (Psalm 69:9). But of great interest here is what Jesus said to the Jews who confronted him and demanded an account for his action. They said to him, "What sign have you to show us for doing this?" In other words, 'who gave you the audacity to re-order things in the temple?' They wanted him to show them a sign that he has got such authority. Jesus simply said to them, "Destroy this temple, and in three days I will raise it up" (John 2:13-23). Of course they took Jesus' word literary and thought he was referring to the physical structure that took their forefathers forty-six years to build. Not knowing that Jesus was referring to his power and dominion over death.

The most they could do was to kill him, but Jesus was not afraid because he knew that he has power over death and will rise again after three days. According to the Bible, "When therefore he was raised from the dead, his disciples remembered that he had said this; and they believed the scripture and the word which Jesus had spoken" (John 2:22).

The resurrection of Jesus Christ is the strongest sign of his dominion over sin and death. This means that his dominion is a life-giving dominion. The scripture attest to this: "Christ has been raised from the dead, the first fruits of those who have fallen asleep.... For as in

Adam all die, so also in Christ shall all be made alive" (Romans 6:4). The Catechism of the Catholic Church also teaches us that "by his death, Christ liberates us from sin; by his Resurrection, he opens for us the way to a new life." This new life is, above all justification, which reinstates us in God's grace, so that as Christ was raised from the dead by the glory of the Father, we too might walk in newness of life. Hence, St Paul will say, "If anyone is in Christ, he is a new creation; the old has passed away, behold, the new has come." So, as Christians, we can be confident that Jesus Christ has won the final victory and is in control of everything that concerns us.

We need not to live in fear anymore; especially the fear of death, since Jesus has conquered death for us. The scriptures are clear about this: "For you did not receive spirit of slavery to fall back into fear, but you have received the spirit of sonship. When we cry, "Abba! Father!"" (Romans 8:15). It is the same thing that St Paul reminded Timothy in his second letter to him, "For this reason I remind you to rekindle the gift of God that is within you through the laying on of my hands; for God did not give us a spirit of timidity but a spirit of power and love and self-control (1:6-7). Christians who live in fear have not yet come to the knowledge and awareness of this power. As a Christian, you don't need to be afraid or live in fear anymore, for you are co-heir with Christ – sharing in his dominion.

Chapter 3
God's Glory and Man's Dominion

"O Lord, our Lord, how majestic is your name in all the earth! You whose glory above the heavens is chanted by the mouth of babies and infants, you have founded a bulwark because of your foes, to still the enemy and the avenger. When I look at your heavens, the work of your fingers, the moon and the stars which you have established; what is man that you are mindful of him, and the son of man that you care for him? Yet you have made him little less than the angels, and you have crowned him with glory and honour. You have given him dominion over the works of your hands; you have put all things under his feet, all sheep and oxen, and also the beasts of the field, the birds of the air, and the fish of the sea, whatever passes along the paths of the sea. O Lord, our Lord, how majestic is your name in all the earth!" (Psalm 8:1-9)

The above text is a hymn in praise of God the creator, whose greatness can be seen from the wonder of the universe that he made. We feel small when we contemplate the immensity of this universe. But in spite of our smallness in comparison to the rest of creation, we have been created in the image of God and are almost equal in dignity to the heavenly beings. To respect God's majesty, we must compare ourselves to his greatness. When we look at creation, we often feel small by comparison. This is a healthy path to reality, but God does not want us to dwell on our smallness. Humility means proper respect for God, not self-deprecation.

When we look at the vast expanse of creation, we wonder how God could be concerned for people who constantly disappoint him. Yet God created us only slightly lower than himself and the angels! The next time you question your worth as a person, remember that God considers you highly valuable. We have great worth because we have the stamp of the Creator. In the creation account we are told, "Then God said, "Let us make humankind in our image, according to our likeness; and let them have dominion over the fish of the sea, and over the birds of the air, and over the cattle, and over all the wild animals of the earth, and over every creeping thing that creeps upon the earth."

So God created humankind in his image, in the image of God he created them; male and female he created them" (Genesis 1:26-27). This is a clear evidence of the kind of worth that God has placed on us. We are valuable to him, consequently, we need to extricate ourselves from the feelings of worthlessness.

In Zechariah 2:8, "For thus said the Lord of host ... Truly, one who touches you touches the apple of my eye." When Jesus in the Gospel of Matthew addressed his followers on the need not to worry he said, "Look at the birds of the air; they neither sow nor reap nor gather into bands, and yet your heavenly Father feeds them. Are you not of more value than they?" (6:26). My dear friend, stop looking down on yourself – you've got some stuff inside of you. And you are of great value before your creator. Talking about the spirit of anti-christ that is already in the world, the scripture says, "Little children, you are of God, and have overcome them; for he who is in you is greater than he who is in the world" (1 John 4:4).

A question to ponder upon is: What is it that defines you as a person? From where do you derive your self-worth - from what you do or from who you are? Base on life experience, study and observation, when people are young, they tend to define themselves mostly by what they do. But in the evening or towards the evening of one's life, one is expected to define oneself based on whom one has become. According to psychological analysis in the light of spirituality, none of the definitions is wrong; they only represent the different seasons or stages of life (Rolheiser, 2014). As an adolescent, defining yourself by the things you do is not a problem. But everything is wrong when you are in late adulthood, and still cannot be proud of whom you have become. This is where fixation sets in; a situation whereby one has not been able to outgrow a particular stage in one's development. Life is stages, and every physically and spiritually matured Christian should have a true sense of self-worth, not allowing things to define you, but knowing who you have become in Christ. As St. Paul would say, "When I was a child, I spoke like a child, I thought like a child, I reasoned like a child; when I became a man, I gave up childish ways" (1 Corinthians 13:11).

God gave human beings tremendous authority – to be in charge of the whole earth. Imagine this – "You have given him dominion over the works of your hands; you have put all things under his feet…" We have more powers than we are able to comprehend. The inability to comprehend this power is the root cause of most of our problems, be they psychological, spiritual, economical, physical and otherwise. We need to be conscious of this enormous power that God has deposited in us as his children. We also need to nurture it because with great power and authority comes great responsibility. If, for example, you own a pet, you have the legal authority to do with it as you wish, but you also have the responsibility to feed and care for it.

Chapter 4
Arise and Take Dominion

The true light that enlightens every man was coming into the world. He was in the world, and the world was made through him, yet the world knew him not. He came to his own home, and his own people received him not. But to all who received him, who believed in his name, he gave power to become children of God; who were born not of blood nor of the will of the flesh nor of the will of man, but of God (John 1:9-13).

To all who received him, who believed in his name, he gave power to become children of God. In other words, to all who receive Jesus Christ and believe in him as the Messiah and Saviour of the world, have been given the power to be like Chris the only begotten Son of the Father. Such people are called to share in his divine nature and dominion over the world. St Peter in his second letter affirmed this when he said, "His divine power has granted to us all things that pertain to life and godliness, through the knowledge of him who called us to his own glory and excellence, by which he has granted to us his precious and very great promises, that through these you may escape from the corruption that is in the world because of passion, and become partakers of the divine nature (2 Peter 1:3-4). This is the power we have in Christ as baptized Christians. In Christ we are richly blessed with the grace of self-control, and the ability to relate with created things in the way and manner that is pleasing to God. Through Christ, we have victory over sin, shame and death. Hence, we are called to live in the light of this victory, without fear, that wells into eternal life with God. The problem today is that a lot of Christians are yet to know the power they have, or the grace that has been made available for them in Christ.

Arising and taking dominion is coming to the knowledge of the power you have in Christ as a Christian, and putting it to use. It means being conscious of the fact that by the virtue of your baptism in Christ, that you have become a co-heir with Christ, and as such, can freely, willingly and constantly tap into Christ's victory over the world and enjoy his dominion. Thus, you come to the knowledge and believe that if Christ was able to overcome temptations, you too can also overcome by his grace and power that is in you. If Christ was able to withstand difficult times and at the end won salvation for the whole world, you too, through his power and grace working in you, can also shoulder every storm of life and come out victorious, with your head high, for your good and the benefit of your family and community.

It is also important to constantly remember that Christ came to restore everything we lost through Adam and Eve. And one of those is our power and dominion over other creatures, and created things. The scripture in Genesis 1:28 says, "And God blessed them, and God said to them, "Be fruitful and multiply, and fill the earth and subdue it; and have dominion over the fish of the sea and over the birds of the air and over every living thing that moves upon the earth." Then, in Chapter 9:2, it goes on to say, "The fear of you and the dread of you shall be upon every beast of the earth, and upon every bird of the air, upon everything that creeps on the ground and all the fish of the sea; into your hand they are delivered". We lost all these with the fall of Adam and Eve, but we found and rediscover them in Christ. So in Christ, you are to ARISE AND TAKE DOMINION!

You are to take dominion over everything that God has given to you both in the spiritual, and in the physical realms. You are to take dominion over your spiritual life, physical health, material wealth and finances. You are to take charge of your family, work or business, and everything that concerns you by bringing them under the power of Christ. What an authority, power and control has God given to us! In making use of this power, you can close every door through which the devil may want to attack and devour your blessings. So arise and take dominion in every aspect of your life. That is, 360 degrees dominion. This power is yours in Christ. Speak blessing into the life of your kids, bless your spouse, speak life into a business that is about to collapse, prophesy breakthrough and increase into your family, pray down healing upon a sick child, sister, brother, parent or friend. It is the same power that can help you to overcome a bad habit, and set you free from being an addict.

What authority, power, and control has God given to us! But some people are yet to realize this enormous power that has been made available to us. Jesus confirmed this when he said, "For truly, I say to you, if you have faith as a grain of mustard seed, you will say to this mountain, 'Move from here to there,' and it will move; and nothing will be impossible to you" (Matthew 17:20). Some find it difficult to take charge of their life circumstances and subject them to the Ultimate Power of God because they are yet to realize that they have the power to do so. So, this lack of realization is causing this power to lie dormant in them, untapped and unused. Unfortunately, when you fail to tap into this gratuitous power of God, you will suffer a great deal of deprivation. Thus, things that are to be controlled by you will end up controlling you.

Some people, today, are controlled not just by some spiritual demons, but also by the demon of materialism which plays itself out in different forms: money, drugs, alcohol, indiscriminate sex, masturbation, anger, inordinate fashion, and internet fever - excessive and endless time on the net to the point that they can't stay offline for a few hours without feeling sick. The truth is, all these things are meant to be under our control if we would only rise and take dominion. Two things facilitate our ability to rise and take dominion: (1) understanding who you are in Christ and (2) laying hold of his promises.

1. Understand Who You Are in Christ

In John 1:12 the scripture says, "To all who received him, who believed in his name, he gave power to become children of God." This refers to all those who have accepted Jesus as Lord - people baptized into the life and death of Jesus Christ, who constantly profess faith in him; people who are not ashamed or afraid to witness for him before unbelievers. To these people he said the power is given to become the children of God. Do you know what it means to be a child of God? If yes, then be sure that you have understood whom you have become in Christ Jesus. Otherwise, you need to dig deep for this understanding. This understanding will blow your mind, it will change your worldview, and it will liberate and empower you beyond your imagination. This is why Christ came. He said, "The thief comes only to steal and kill and destroy; I came that they may have life, and have it abundantly" (John 10:10).

Jesus himself knows how much we need this power, that is why even after his ministry on earth, in one of his parting speeches he said, "I will not leave you desolate; I will come to you" (John 14:8), and in Acts of the Apostles 1:8 before the Pentecost, he told his apostles: "You shall receive power when the Holy Spirit has come upon you." We read in the Acts of the Apostles how effective and bold the apostles became afterwards. They became more conscious of whom they have become in Christ, and the power that is at work in them.

It was in this light that St. Paul encouraged Timothy in his new office as a young leader: "For God did not give us a spirit of timidity but a spirit of power and love and self-control" (2 Timothy 1:7). Then, to the Romans he said, "For you did not receive the spirit of slavery to fall back into fear, but you have received the spirit of adoption. When we cry, "Abba! Father" it is that very spirit bearing witness with our spirit that we are children of God, and if children, then heirs, heirs of God and fellow heirs with Christ, provided we suffer with him in order that we may also be glorified with him" (8:15-17). It is important for you to know this, because this is the foundation of your dominion.

The story is told of an African woman whose son travelled abroad. Over the years, the son was sending her dollars, but she didn't know they were legal tender. She mistakenly took them to be gift cards. At a point she became seriously ill and was taken to the hospital by some of her neighbours. She was diagnosed with a serious health problem, and a huge sum was required for her treatment. Knowing fully well that she had been looking wretched since her son left the country, they tried to enquire from her if her son kept in touch.

They were exploring different avenues of raising funds required for her treatment. The woman said, "Yes, from time to time he sends to me some gift cards, which I normally keep under the matrass. Please go to my house and check if any of those cards has his phone number or contact so you can call him for me." On reaching there, it was discovered to everyone amazement that the gift cards were actually $100 bills. The woman was richer than she knew, and was dying of malnutrition and wretchedness. This is what happens when you have something and don't know what you have; and when you don't know what you have, you can never know its value and use.

2. Lay hold of his promises

After you have realized whom you have become in Christ, the next thing is to apply his to your life. God has made a lot of promises in scriptures, especially to those who have come to faith in Jesus Christ. The problem is either that most of the time God's children are not mindful of these promises or that most of us (God's children) are ignorant of them. For example in Mark's gospel 16:17: "And these signs will accompany those who believe: in my name they will cast out demons; they will speak in new tongues; they will pick up serpents, and if they drink any deadly thing, it will not hurt them; they will lay their hands on the sick, and they will recover." What a great promise! Towards the end of his ministry on earth, Jesus also made the following promises: "Very truly, I tell you, the one who believes in me will also do the works that I do and, in fact, will do greater works than these, because I am going to the Father" (John 14:12); "I will not leave you orphaned; I am coming to you" (John 14:18); "I am with you always, to the end of the age" (Matthew 28:20).

These are promises that you must claim to enjoy the dominion that God has given to you as his child. As Children of God, who have become co-heirs with Christ, we have dominion. And our dominion is in Christ Jesus, who in Matthew's Gospel said, "All authority in heaven and on earth has been given to me..." (Matthew 28:18). Our authority is in Christ, and in it we find fulfilment. This prompted St. Paul to state in 2 Corinthians 10:4, "The weapons of our warfare are not merely human, but they have divine power to destroy strongholds."

Dominion is understanding that you can do what God said you can do: God said if you have faith as little as the mustard seed, you can say to this mountain, "move or be uprooted", and it will obey you (Matthew

17:20). He said make a decree and it shall come to pass (Job 22:28).

Dominion is understanding that you can have what God has promised you: God said, "You shall eat the fruit of the labour of your hands; you shall be happy and it shall go well with you." (Isaiah 65:22). "You shall have a wife, and your wife will be like a fruitful vine within your house; your children will be like olive shoots around your table." (Psalm 128:3).

Dominion is understanding that you can realize your God-given potential, regardless of what things look like, sound or appear like: God said, "You will be a lender not a borrower, you will be the head and not the tail; you shall be only at the top, and not at the bottom" (Deuteronomy 28:13). He said, "Truly, one who touches you touches the apple of my eye" (Zachariah 2:8). It is possible that because of the way things are happening in your life, you have given up, or are about to give up. You don't need to give up. You have to ARISE AND TAKE DOMINION by understanding or reminding yourself of whom you have become in Christ and claiming these promises.

Part 2
Principles of Living in Dominion

Living in Dominion requires discipline and the observance of certain moral principles. The seven principles discussed in this second part of the book are the pillars and constitute the tap root upon which this way of life can not only survive but thrive. They are: obedience, holiness, hard work, prayer, divine wisdom, courage and generosity.

Chapter 5
Obedience

Obedience is the willingness to do what one is asked to do. It means submitting to the demands of a legitimate authority be it human or divine. Simply put, it is doing what you are asked to do, by a legitimate authority, without grudges, and possibly without questioning. In most cases, one who demands obedience from you is one who has got the power or authority to do so. This authority could be as a result of the office that the person occupies, knowledge, insight and vision that someone has, or the role that one plays in your life. For example a Prime Minister or the President of a country has got some authority because of the office he or she occupies. Whereas parents have some authority in the family because of their role.

The Church teaches us that a citizen is obliged in conscience not to follow the directives of civil authorities when they are contrary to the demands of the moral order, to the fundamental rights of persons or the teachings of the Gospel (CCC #2242). Refusing obedience to civil authorities, when their demands are contrary to those of an upright conscience finds its justification in the distinction between serving God and serving the political community. The scripture says, "Render therefore to Caesar the things that are Caesar's, and to God the things that are God's" (Matthew 22:21). In the Acts of the Apostles when the early followers of Christ were asked by a civil or human authority not to preach the Gospel, which Jesus Christ gave them the mandate to do, they responded, "We must obey God rather than men" (5:29). So in all things, the authority of God is to come first. St Thomas Aquinas (1225-1274), in his Summa Theologica opined that "God is to be obeyed in all things, while human authorities are to be obeyed in certain things. Obedience to God is without limit, whereas obedience to human beings is limited by higher by-laws that must not be transgressed, and by the competency or authority of the one who gives the orders" (II, II, Question 104, Articles 4 and 5).

The Catechism of the Catholic Church went further to define obedience as a virtue which requires everyone to give due honour to authority and to treat those who are charged to exercise it with respect, and, insofar as it is deserved, with gratitude and good-will (CCC #1900).

Jesus Christ, the Eternal Son of God, obeyed His Father by becoming man through the power of the Holy Spirit and was born of the Virgin Mary, later going to his obedience – inspired salvific death on Calvary. For as by one man's disobedience many were made sinners, so by one man's obedience many will be made righteous. By his obedience unto death, Jesus accomplished the substitution of the suffering servant, who "makes himself an offering for sin," when "he bore the sin of many," and who "shall make many to be accounted righteous," for "he shall bear their iniquities" (Romans 5:18-19). Jesus atoned for our faults and made satisfaction for our sins to the Father.

The reason God demands obedience from us is because he loves us so much, and wants us to constantly make informed choices. Choice for life and not for death, choice for blessings and not for curse, choice for light and not for darkness. As a loving Father, he is always looking out for us, not wanting us to hurt ourselves by the choices we make. God doesn't force his will on anyone; he lets us decide whether to follow him and do his will, or to reject him and do our own will or the will of the evil one – Satan. God demands obedience from us for our own good; out of the love he has for us. He always wants the best for us. Though some see his demand as infringing on their right. But he gave you the right in the first place. God's purpose for demanding obedience from his children is not to enslave us, but to keep us safe. We obey rules in the society for the sake of order and peaceful co-existence. Likewise, we need to obey God for order in our life. So, to live in dominion is to choose to obey Him in all things; putting his will first before any human will. Thereby, enjoying an ordered life that is balance; physically, psychologically, socially and spiritually.

It is profiting and very beneficial to be obedient to God. The scripture is very clear on this, "And if you obey the voice of the Lord your God, being careful to do all his commandments which I command you this day, the Lord your God will set you high above all the nations of the earth" (Deuteronomy 28:1). We find obedient quite challenging; be it common instructions by human institutions or constituted authority, or the commandment of God. Some people have gone to the extent of saying that the human person is naturally rebellious possibly as a result of the Eden experience. We know the story too well: the sin of our first parents was the sin of disobedience.

The Church refers to it as Original Sin. Adam and Eve were told not to eat of the tree in the middle of the garden (Genesis 3:3). And as long as they obeyed this commandment of God, they stayed in the garden and enjoyed the friendship of God. They were in charge of all the other creatures, and lived a happy life, a life free of stress, depression, backbiting, nagging, the pain of childbirth and all other life threatening problems which constitute our lot today. But after they disobeyed, it was a total turn around. This marked the beginning of human suffering and pain (Genesis 3:14-19). The Church, however, calls it a Happy Fault because it necessitated the coming of the redeemer – Jesus Christ.

Going through the scriptures and Church history, it is obvious that most of the heroes of our faith were very obedient people. And many who failed, failed largely as a result of disobedience. It is either they disobeyed the commandments of God, the teachings of his Church or constituted authority – the hierarchy of the Church. To live in dominion, we must be obedient people; obedient to the will of God and obedient to those in authority. Nevertheless, when the directives of those in authority are contrary to the will of God, the demands of the moral order, and to the fundamental rights of persons or the teachings of the Gospel, we are to remember that obedience to God comes first. (CCC #2242). We must obey God rather than man (Acts 5:29).

Chapter 6
Holiness

A person living in dominion needs some moral power, this comes through holiness of life. Jesus as always is a perfect example, "And they were astonished at his teaching, for he taught them as one who had authority, and not as the scribes" (Mark 1:22; Matthew 7:28-29). When Jesus taught in the synagogues and in the countryside during the course of his ministry on earth, his teachings made a deep impression on the people, unlike that of the scribes. The scripture says, he taught them with authority. Jesus' teaching with authority is not simply because he is God's son; but also because his life style was at one with his preaching. When we profess one thing and do another, we fall short of this moral power. Holiness of life is one thing that can help us sustain this moral power. The Lord spoke to Moses, "Say to all the congregation of the sons of Israel, you shall be holy; for I the Lord your God am holy"

(Leviticus 19:1-2). Why? Because that is how they can maintain the Spiritual Dominion that he gave to them.

Unfortunately, today people struggle not with holiness per se, but with their concept of holiness. As such, many are afraid to talk about it. A priest friend of mine who was sent on mission came to a parish, and after six months, he preached on "Holiness of Life". At the end of the Mass, a parishioner came to him and said, "Father, thank you for today's sermon. For the past 18 years that I have been in this parish, no one has ever talked about Holiness." Of course the priest was deeply shocked, which explains one of the reasons he narrated the experience to me. This also confirms Matthew Kelly's assertion in his book, "Rediscover Catholicism", that a great number of priests and teachers stopped preaching, teaching and speaking about holiness because they felt it is an unrealistic goal. So, they wanted to make it easier for people and possibly eradicate guilt feelings which they assumed results from it. But unknown to them, they watered down the great goal of the Christian life.

Holiness does not mean being in a sinless state. Otherwise, the only one that would be worthy of it would be Jesus Christ whom the scripture says is like us in all things except sin (Hebrews 4:15). Even then, when he was addressed as "Good Teacher", he retorted, "Why do you call me good? No one is good but God alone." (Mark 10:17-18). This is Jesus speaking humanly. Every human person is still in the process of becoming; there is always a room for improvement, learning and growth. So, holiness is not a state but a conscious process and effort towards attaining the Highest Good. Holiness of life is simply struggling towards perfection. Thus, Jesus admonishes us – "You, therefore, must be perfect, as your heavenly Father is perfect." (Matthew 5:48). He knows that we are imperfect beings, full of imperfections, limitations and brokenness. But he want us to maintain a relentless effort towards God.

There is a story I love so much in the Bible that drives this message home so well. It is about Jonah and the people of Nineveh. After Jonah's attempt to flee from God, his encounter in the belly of the fish, and a later change of heart to go on the errand that God sent him (Jonah 1 & 2), the scripture says:

> Then the word of the Lord came to Jonah the second time, saying, "Arise, go to Nineveh, that great city, and proclaim to it the message that I tell you." So Jonah arose and went to Nineveh,

according to the word of the Lord. Now Nineveh was an exceedingly great city, three days' journey in breadth. Jonah began to go into the city, going a day's journey. And he cried, "Yet forty days, and Nineveh shall be overthrown!" And the people of Nineveh believed God; they proclaimed a fast, and put on sackcloth, from the greatest of them to the least of them. Then tidings reached the king of Nineveh, and he arose from his throne, removed his robe, and covered himself with sackcloth, and sat in ashes. And he made proclamation and published through Nineveh, "By the degree of the king and his nobles: Let neither man nor beast, herd nor flock, taste anything; let them not feed, or drink water, but let man and beast be covered with sackcloth, and let them cry mightily to God; yes let everyone turn from his evil way and from the violence which is in his hands. Who knows, God may yet

repent and turn from his fierce anger,
so that we perish not?" (Jonah 3:1-9).

When you read the last verse (10), which is the portion I love so much, it says that when God saw their effort, he relented from the wrath he had wanted to inflict upon them. So, it is not about being sinless; it is about daily struggle towards righteousness, making sincere effort, falling into sin and not remaining in sin but getting up immediately to continue the struggle. St. Paul captured this so well when he said, "Put off the old man that belongs to your former manner of life and is corrupt through deceitful lusts, and be renewed in the spirit of your minds, and put on the new man, created after the likeness of God in true righteousness and holiness" (Ephesians 4:22-24). As one living in dominion, you have to constantly make an effort to clothe yourself with the likeness of God - in words and in action.

Always ask the Lord for a Forgiving Spirit, which is equally important in the pursuit of holiness. This means the ability to let go when you are being hurt or offended. This ability is an attribute of the strong. So, as someone who is living in dominion, you must have a forgiving spirit. It gives you an edge, and keeps you in charge.

Chapter 7
Hard Work

By hard work I mean being diligent with your work. Doing it well with commitment and in all honesty. It is possible that you are employed by someone, or you are self-employed, or possible still that you have a vocation. In any case, it is worth doing diligently; that is, keeping up with the demands of your job. One of the signs of living in dominion is diligence at work. You don't lazy around, but you do your work with devotion. The scripture says, "Whatever your hand finds to do, do it with your might; for there is no work or thought of knowledge or wisdom in Sheol to which you are going" (Ecclesiastes 9:10). When I see people not taking their job seriously, it baffles me. This is because the job that someone is not serious about, another person some-where or some place, possibly in another region, state/province or even country, is dying and praying to God day and night to have. According to the statistics released by Gallup in 2013, only 13 percent of people worldwide actually like going to work. This 13 percent of employees are said to be "engaged" in their jobs, or emotionally invested in their work and focused on helping their organisation improve (McGregor, 2013). So, what about the other 87%?

Research has shown that 63 percent are "not engaged" – or simply unmotivated and unlikely to exert extra effort – while the remaining 24 percent are "actively disengaged", or truly unhappy and unproductive (McGregor, 2013). This categorize workers that are always complaining about their job, as if they are forced to do it. Some do their work with a carefree attitude; disrespecting and insulting people all the way. Sometimes when I look at such people, I'm tempted to just offer a Mass for them for the grace to be out of a job/business (unemployed), for a year or two, hoping that such a period of grace will help them come to terms with their job and appreciate it better. But on a second thought, I decided to research into why people don't like what they do as job, or hate their work. In the course of my research, I stumbled on the publication of Liz Ryan (2016), which explored the ten top reasons people hate their jobs. She opined:

1. They are not respected as people at work. They are viewed as production units, rather than valued collaborators.

2. They don't have the right tools, equipment, information and basic operational requirements they need to do their jobs, then their employers get mad at them for asking?

3. Their employer disregards their personal life and has no compassion for their obligations outside of work.

4. Their immediate supervisor is either a tyrant, unqualified for their job, or both.

5. They are tired of being lied to.

6. They have no vision for the future and no confidence their leaders will do the right thing, either from a business standpoint or human standpoint.

7. They are tired of dealing with the politics in their workplace

8. They are underpaid and overworked.

9. They go to work every day and push a rock uphill, trying in vain to get forward motion on their projects. They are tired of pushing.

10. They have to watch every word they say and every move they make, because the knives are out and

they could get in trouble – or get fired – for almost any reason.

In as much as the above appear to be reasonable, you have the power as the employee to either enjoy the job as the only one that is available at the time, or quit the job for one that you have passion for. Certain times, if not most of the times, it is not the paycheque but the passion you have for the job that will keep you. If you are happy with what you do, people know. They feel it because it rubs off on them positively. Likewise, when you grumble in your work always, people also perceive the negativity. But as one living in dominion, it is compulsory to do your work well. The Church captures this so well when it states:

> Human work, whether it is done independently or as an employee, proceeds from the human person, who as it were, puts a personal seal on the things of nature and reduces them to her or his will. By their work people ordinarily provide for themselves and their family, associate with others as their brothers and sisters, and serve them; they can exercise a genuine charity and be partners in the work of bringing

God's creation to perfection (Gaudium
et Spes, #67).

Work was created by God, and should be appreciated
for what it is. Besides being a source of livelihood, it is
our means of perfecting God's creation. As such, we are
to work with all dedication. To show how serious it is,
St. Paul in his Second Letter to the Thessalonians exerts,
"Now we command you, brethren, in the name of our
Lord Jesus Christ that you keep away from any brother
who is walking in idleness and not in accord with the
tradition that you received from us. For you yourselves
know how you ought to imitate us; we were not idle
when we were with you, we did not eat anyone's bread
without paying, but with toil and labour we worked night
and day, that we might not burden any of you. It was not
because we have not that right, but to give you in our
conduct an example to imitate. For even when we were
with you, we gave you this command: If anyone will not
work, let him not eat" (6-10). It is as simple as that.

It is pertinent that when you are old enough to work
and you are not working, you become burden to yourself and unto others. One who is created by God to live
in dominion is not supposed to be a burden. In this
vein, my elder brother Sunday, used to say to us when
we try to be mischievous as emerging adults, "At this

stage in life, you should be a solution not a problem". I think he has a point. One who has attained the age to work and make a living should not be idling about and still be doing childish things. Instead the story should be like that of St. Paul - "When I was a child, I spoke like a child, I thought like a child, I reasoned like a child; when I became a man, I gave up childish ways" (1 Corinthians 13:11). Work is created by God, and even his only begotten Son worked. Moreover, we believe by faith that through our work, offered to God, humanity is associated with the redemptive work of Jesus Christ, whose labour with his hands at Nazareth greatly added to the dignity of work (Gaudium et Spes, #67). The introductory rite of the order for the blessing of an office, shop, or factory captured this so well. It reads:

In his own life Christ Jesus clearly showed us the dignity of labour. When he became incarnate, the Word of the Father was known as the carpenter's son and willingly worked with the tools of his trade. By working with his own hands he transformed toil from being an inherited curse for sin into a source of blessings. It went further to say that, if we do our work well, whatever it may be, and offer it to God, we purify ourselves and through the labour of

***our hands and minds we build up God's creation.
Our work enables us to practice charity and to
help the less fortunate, so that, joined to Christ the
Redeemer, we grow in his love.***

So when you wake up every morning and find work to do, give thanks and praise to God Almighty. Appreciate your work with gratitude to God. Your commitment and dedication to duty should testify to the fact that you appreciate your work. Give your best to your work with cheerfulness, and avoid procrastination. Let that which can be accomplished today not be pushed over, for tomorrow will come with enough concerns. When you appreciate your work through commitment and dedication, you will accomplish a lot. Files will not pile up on your table while people are waiting and getting frustrated because their files have not been attended to, and they are yet to get a response from you.

No one is asking you to do more than a day's job; if every employed person will do enough for the day to justify his or her wages, the world will be a better place and it will have valuable work to show. When you are tired, take a break and come back. If you are sick, ask for a sick leave and go treat yourself so that whenever you are at your duty post, you will be productive. If you are an employer, in addition to your personal diligence, you are to create a conducive working environment and condition for your employees. Otherwise, when they don't deliver, you are partly responsible.

It is God's design that we should be hard working, and enjoy the blessings or fruit that comes with our labour. He made a solemn promise to his people: "They shall build houses and inhabit them; they shall plant vineyards and eat their fruit. They shall not build and another inhabit; they shall not plant and another eat; for like days of a tree shall the days of my people be, and my chosen shall long enjoy the work of their hands" (Isaiah 65:21-22). God wants us not only to work, but also to enjoy the fruit of our work. As people called to live in dominion, our attitude to work should be a godly attitude.

Chapter 8
Prayer

As a child, I was taught in Catechism that prayer is the lifting up of our heart and mind to God. But as an adult, I see prayer, simply, as a relationship with God. I once said to the kids in my parish that praying in the morning when you wake up from sleep is like going to dad's room to say, "Good morning daddy", or into grandpa's room to check on him; to see how he is doing and have a good chat with him. In the same manner, Henry Nouwen (1986), considered prayer to be a movement, whereby one reaches out to God. He said, "It is through this movement that we reach out to God, our God, the one who is eternally real and from whom all reality comes forth" (P. 114). Prayer is a relational art of reaching out and remaining connected to God, the divine source of all we have and are.

Some people find it difficult to pray; not because they don't want to pray, or don't know the importance of prayer. The difficulty is on how to construct their prayer. It is important to note that you don't need to be a good speech maker or a good poem/song composer to pray. God, as a loving Father, wants you to come to Him as you are. You can come to him with the traditionally written prayers like the Lord's Prayer, you can also come to him with spontaneous prayers. In spontaneous prayers, you can use the Lord's Prayer as a pattern and come to God in your own words: Thanking Him for his goodness, asking for his mercy, protection from evil, and telling Him about your concerns and that of your family and friends. You let him know the areas of your life where you need strength and support, and ask him for the blessings that you need. Just the way you will chat or discuss with your earthly father. Share your feelings with Him, the same way you will with your earthly father. If you feel like crying go ahead and cry in His presence. If you are excited about something, tell Him you are… you don't need fancy words or super composure to be able to pray. All you need is the consciousness of God's presence.

This consciousness of the divine presence is very important because to live in Spiritual Dominion, you must be very prayerful – Constantly connected to God. Jesus is a good example for us of a prayerful life. He stayed connected to the Father through prayers in the course of his earthly ministry. He prayed in season and out of season; not just in every given circumstance, but in different occasions as recorded in the scriptures:

"And in the morning, a great while before day, he rose and went out to a lonely place, and there he prayed" (Mark 1:35). This brings to mind the idea of beginning each day with prayer. Don't begin your day without a conscious pause to connect with the divine and hand over the day to God.

"At that time Jesus declared, "I thank you , Father, Lord of heaven and earth, that you have hidden these things from the wise and understanding and revealed them to infants; yes, Father, for such was your gracious will"" (Matthew 11:25-26). Here, in the midst of the day's event, Jesus paused to give thanks and praise to God the Father. An acknowledgment of His presence in his experiences. We too are to constantly pause from our activities to give God praise and thanks as we see his hand in the unfolding of the day's activity or work. When exciting and surprising things happen around us in the course of the day, they should occasion a pause for thanksgiving and praise to God.

"In these days he went out to the hills to pray; and all night he continued in prayer to God" (Luke 6:12). This brings to mind the significance of night vigil with the Lord. This was shortly before Jesus chose the Twelve Disciples. Thus, he set out time and prayed specially. He denied himself sleep, and spent the whole night discussing with the Father on how he will go about this task of getting people to work with him. Don't make any major decision in your life without first of all setting aside time to pray and reflect about it, and allow the Spirit of God to lead you and give you counsel.

"Now is my soul troubled. And what shall I say? 'Father, save me from this hour'? No, for this purpose I have come to this hour. Father, glorify your name. Then a voice came from heaven, "I have glorified it, and I will glorify it again" (John 12:27-28). This is Jesus praying to the Father in the time of trouble and distress; in the time of pain, worries and anxiety. When we are in similar situations, we are to look up to God in prayer for strength, support and direction like he did.

"So they took away the stone. And Jesus lifted up his eyes and said, "Father, I thank you that you have heard me. I knew that you always hear me, but I have said this on account of the people standing by, that they may believe that you sent me"" (John 11:41-42). This is one of Jesus' prayer of thanksgiving to the Father for answering his prayer. How often do we forget to thank God for request granted unto us?

From the foregoing biblical passages, it is evident that Jesus prayed in all seasons: He prayed first thing in the morning; thereby beginning each day with prayer. He offered prayers of thanksgiving at different occasions; appreciating God for divine revelation, and answered prayers. More so, Jesus prayed before major decisions in his life and when he was in distress. That is the open secret of the Dominion of Jesus Christ – He stayed connected to the Father through prayers. As people called to live in dominion, we must cultivate the life of prayer. We are to pray like Jesus did.

You should pray in season and out of season because everything material was first spiritual before God brought it into being. It existed first in the mind of God before it was produced in the physical realm. In prayers, you take charge of things in the spiritual realm, before their physical manifestation, so that when they begin to happen, the situation will be to your advantage. The scripture says, "Do not worry about anything, but in everything by prayer and supplication with thanksgiving let your requests be made known to God" (Philippians 4:6). Admonishing the Colossians, St. Paul also laid the same emphasis when he wrote, "Continue steadfastly in prayer, being watchful in it with thanksgiving (Colossians 4:2). No wonder Matthew Kelly in his book, "Rediscover Catholicism", opined that, "Prayer is central to the Christian experience. A Christian life is not sustainable without it, because growth in the Christian life is simply not possible without prayer. Growing in character and virtue, learning to hear the voice of God in our lives and walking where he calls us – all require the discipline of prayer" (2010: pp. 170).

Prayer, as a matter of fact, should be part and parcel of the life of a child of God, who wants to live in dominion and take charge of the things happening around him or her. You do not pray only when you need favour from God or want him to deliver you from a predicament. Otherwise, you will be turning prayer into crisis-related activity, or a support system that is employed when you can no longer help yourself (Nouwen, 1986). A true child of God living in dominion prays in season and out of season as recommended by St. Paul (1 Thessalonians 5:17). He prays because he understands the value of prayer. He knows that prayer keeps him connected to the heavenly realm, where most decisions are made about earthly beings/things.

Life, no doubt, is full of ups and downs. One way to stem the tide and wait out the storms of life is to be a "praying mantis". In Luke's Gospel, while on the Mount of Olives, Jesus said to the disciples, "Pray that you may not enter into temptation" (22:40). In other words, if temptations are bound to come as part of human existence, they should always meet us praying and prepared. It makes a lot of difference when problems meet you already in the spirit. Such problems won't sweep you off your feet. You will be better prepared to handle them. Your response in speech and action will be well calculated and guided by the spirit of God. As such, you will get the enemy confused, because what the enemy will see, will not meet his expectation. The trial that they thought will kill you, or make you say things that will cause you your job, position in the office, relationship, and the like will come and leave you better than they met you. You will still be smiling and happy because you are constantly in touch with the divine. God's word will be fulfilled in you that says, "When they deliver you up, do not be anxious about how you are to speak or what you are to say; for what you are to say will be given to you in that hour" (Matthew 10:19). The prayerful Christian can be compared to the righteous in Psalm 112:7, "He is not afraid of evil tidings; his heart is firm, trusting in the Lord". And he may have or face many troubles, but the Lord delivers him from them all (Psalm 34:19). It is all about 24/7 connection with the divine. Look at this, Jesus told his disciples a parable, to the effect that they ought always to pray and not lose heart:

> He said, "In a certain city there was a judge who neither feared God nor regarded man; and there was a widow in that city who kept coming to him and saying, 'Vindicate me against my adversary.' For a while he refused; but afterward he said to himself, 'Though I neither fear God nor regard man, yet because this widow bothers me, I will vindicate her, or she will wear me out by her continual coming.' And the Lord said, "Hear what the unrighteous judge says. And will not God vindicate his elect, who cry to him day and night? Will he delay long over them? I tell you, he will vindicate them speedily... (Luke 18:1-8).

Wow! Let the problems of life meet you praying. As such, you will come out stronger, better, experienced, and more courageous to face the ones ahead. Moreover, prayer will not only empower you to always be in charge, it will help you dictate pit-falls so that you can avoid them and never sink or go down.

Testimony on the Power of Prayer

Between August 2010 and November 2012, I served as the Cathedral Administrator in Kano Diocese. This was the period when the Radical Islamic group – Boko Haram insurgency was at its peak in Northern Nigeria. The most co-ordinated attack of this group on the ancient city of Kano was carried out on January 20, 2012. Before this unforgettable day, I had taken some days off from the parish. I left the parish shortly before New Year, and came back on January 5. But as I drove into the rectory (Parish House) and stepped out of my car, I sensed a strange atmosphere that was equally unwelcoming. This was quite unusual. Whenever I was away, I longed to go back home, to my own bed and space. But on this day it was different. Immediately I felt the urge to pray. I took it upon myself to begin a seven days prayer from the next day being Friday.

During this seven days of prayer and fasting, on Tuesday of the following week, a woman came to see me in the office and said, "Father, I had a dream about you, and what I saw was terrible. I will advise that you offer Masses for yourself, and if possible fast and pray for seven days." She also gave to me some Psalms that she felt I should pray. I thanked her and she left. After she left, I continued with other businesses of the day, because this is a very busy Church. But during my quiet time, I ran through all that she said once again in my head. Then, the battle became, "But you are already doing a seven-day fasting and prayer, is that not enough?" Thank goodness, at the end of the day, I resolved to begin the prayer she recommended immediately I finished the one I was doing already. And that was exactly what happened. I ended the one I initiated by myself on January 13, and I started hers on the 14th.

However, on the Thursday the 12th, my iPhone 4 fell down and the screen was completely damaged. I kept it aside and started using my old Nokia phone. I never wanted the damaged phone to cause me any bitterness or distraction. Surprisingly, on Friday, January 20, 2012, during my lunch break, I came into the room and laid down for my usual nap. But after a minute or two, I stood up from the bed, picked up the shattered iPhone, and thought: "Why not go and fix it?" A gentle voice said to me, "But this is not part of your schedule for the day". Hearing this gentle voice, I dropped the phone and laid back again, and immediately fell asleep. It was in the course of this sleep that the Boko Haram attack took place. In fact, I woke up to the phone call from one of my associate priests, who alerted me on the situation. Immediately, I woke up and went to the Church and started directing my staff, the security outfit and parishioners who were already in the Church waiting for the evening Mass.

The point is this: Through prayer and fasting, God prepared me ahead of time for the crisis. Miraculously too, God stopped me from stepping out that afternoon. It might interest you to know that the very place where I would have taken the iPhone to for repairs was one of the places that was terribly attacked that day. Besides that, I was filled with divine wisdom and courage that helped me stay on top of things: To give out constructive instructions that helped us stay safe that day in the Cathedral and even beyond. When I was leaving the Cathedral for a study leave and mission in Canada, someone sent me this message:

Dear Fr, even though I know you will be transferred one day, I didn't know you will leave us so soon. I want you to know that you have written your name in Gold, not only in OLF {i.e. Our Lady of

Fatima – the name of the Church}, but in Kano Diocese as the youngest Very Reverend. You touched many souls spiritually and practically. Yes Fr, YOU NEED THE STUDIES to be spiritually stronger. You indeed need a break from busy OLF. We will miss you, but each time I enter OLF I will say God bless Fr Mbah for keeping the Church together during the turbulent period. May God guide you and fill you with His Grace wherever you go in Jesus name {Amen!}.

The appropriate response to this commendation and prayer is to bow in humility and say - Amen! It's the Lord's doing, and it's marvellous in our sight (Psalm 118:23). If not for God, through prayer, none of that would have been possible or achievable.

Paul Coutinho, in his book titled, "Just As You Are", talks about three paradigms of prayer: (1) from talking to silence, (2) stages of love, relationship and (3) mind, heart and consciousness. Reflecting on the third stage (heart, mind and consciousness), he said, "God does draw a person into a relationship through a person's mind. A person reflects on the scriptures, on spiritual writings, on life experiences, on the social sciences and pure sciences and then formulates a philosophy or a theology." This for him is the prayer of the mind. "The prayer of the heart," he says, "is where God is revealed to us through our feelings, and our prayer is one of appreciation and gratitude for the gifts and blessings we receive. In this way of praying we open ourselves to the mystery of God and the mystery of life and allow that mystery to fill us and transform us into the very mystery we are praying about." Ann Voskamp (2010), confirmed and expressed the same idea and belief when she said that for prayer to be prayer and have any power to change anything, it must first express thanksgiving. So, our prayers should always begin with thanksgiving (Philippians 4:6), acknowledging God for his goodness and kindness towards us, his children, the sheep of his flock, called to live in dominion.

Chapter 9
Divine Wisdom

Divine wisdom is deeper than the intellectual powers of man. It is more than foresight, shrewdness, keenness, insight, and comprehensiveness. The noblest and truest definition of divine wisdom is given in James 3:17-18 which states, "But the wisdom from above is first pure, then peaceable, gentle, open to reason, full of mercy and good fruits, without uncertainty or insincerity" (James 3: 17). It is that wise ability that enables you to coordinate things around you, and manage people and relationships to the glory of God. "Wisdom is one of the weapons that God equips his people with, to enable them to subdue the earth and have dominion over it; just the same way God has dominion over the whole universe" (Adelaja, 2015).

As one living in dominion, you need wisdom from above. As such, you need to pursue wisdom and seek it out. And the best source of wisdom is the Word of God. Seeking wisdom is all about trying to know the truth, so that you don't make conclusions on the basis of assumption. The scriptures says, "You will know the truth, and the truth will make you free" (John 8:32). Divine Wisdom, no doubt, is a gift that is offered freely by God. It is also possible that some are born with it naturally, like King Solomon: "And God gave Solomon wisdom and understanding beyond measure, and largeness of mind like the sand on the seashore, so that Solomon's wisdom surpassed the wisdom of all the people of the east, and all the wisdom of Egypt" (1 Kings 4:29-30).

However, in so many cases one must pray and work hard to acquire divine wisdom. "If any of you lacks wisdom, let him ask God, who gives to all men generously and without reproaching, and it will be given him" (James 1:5). So, one needs to pray, study the scriptures, read books, go for seminars, and carry out research to acquire and increase in divine wisdom. The scripture says, "Buy truth, and do not sell it; buy wisdom, instruction, and understanding" (Proverbs 23:23). Professionals strive to update themselves through reading books in their field of endeavour. Likewise as children of God, called to live in dominion, we are to strive for wisdom from above. The scripture says, "Blessed are those who hunger and thirst for righteousness, for they shall be satisfied" (Matthew 5:6). When we make a sincere effort towards gaining wisdom, God who is always faithful to his promises, has guaranteed us fulfilment and satisfaction. All we need to do is SEEK!

Chapter 10
Courage

You must be courageous. You don't have to live in fear, for fear is not of God and brings about stagnation. It deters you and stops you from going to where you will succeed. If there is one thing that God demands constantly of his children, it is for them to be strong and courageous in the face of hardships and difficulties. God never promised anyone that it will be easy or rosy. But one thing he did promise is that he will not leave us alone or abandon us in the face of problems and life's challenges. When Moses was handing over the mantle of leadership to Joshua, one of the things he stressed again and again is courage.

Moses, at the age of 120, knew that his days on earth were numbered, and the Promised Land was still not in sight. There were still enormous challenges to surmount before his people could get into this land of promise. Since Moses would no longer go with them to finish the journey, the tendency was for them to become discouraged and feel forsaken. But Moses asked them to "Be strong and of good courage, do not fear or be in dread of them: for it is the Lord your God who goes with you; he will not fail you or forsake you" (Deuteronomy 31:6). So, at this point, Moses clearly turned the focus of his folks from himself to the God whom he represented.

Though the physical presence of Moses has always been a source of inspiration to them, Moses made them to understand that it had been the invisible God working through him all the way. And he never forsakes his own or ever gets tired. When Zion felt forsaken and forgotten, the Lord asked them, "Can a woman forget her sucking child, that she should have no compassion on the son of her womb? Even these may forget, yet I will not forget you. Behold, I have graven you on the palms of my hands; your walls are continually before me" (Isaiah 49:14-16). Jesus repeated the same promise when he said, "I am with you always to the close of the age" (Matthew 28:20). These promises are meant to make us courageous as the children of the Most High God.

Whatever you are called to do, wherever you have been placed to function, you can't go far if you lack courage. Once you are living, acting and functioning in fear, your life is half gone. Before long, you would have lost track. St Paul reminded Timothy of this when he wrote to him, "For this reason I remind you to rekindle the gift of God that is within you through the laying on of my hands; for God did not give us a spirit of timidity but a spirit of power and love and self-control" (2 Timothy 1:6-7). In other words, to live in dominion, you need to be in charge; and to be in charge, you need to be courageous as a result of the Spirit of God dwelling in you. So, I should warn you – THE LORD MUST BE YOUR SOURCE OF COURAGE!

Any other source of courage is fleeting. If you make drugs, marijuana, cocaine, and alcohol your source of courage, then you are in for trouble because it will not be you acting, but a substance acting in you. And what happens when there are challenges in front of you waiting to be confronted, and your stimulant is not within reach? Then, you will crash like the house that is built upon sand (Matthew 7:24-27). When the Lord is your source of courage, you can be high every day of the week because he is always within reach.

In Psalm 118:6, the psalmist says, "With the Lord on my side I do not fear. What can mortals do to me?" That is the song or declaration of one who trusts in God as one's source of strength and courage. We saw a demonstration of courage when the king of Assyria Sennach'erib invaded Judah. One of the things that Hezekiah did to remedy the situation was to gather the people and speak courage into them. He said to them, "Be strong and of good courage. Do not be afraid or dismayed before the king of Assyria and all the horde that is with him; for there is one greater with us than with him" (2 Chronicles 32:7). The modern day "King of Assyria" could be someone trying to take away your possessions, or trying to unseat you in your office, or demean you, and doing everything within his or her power to pull you down and to make sure that you don't succeed. FEAR NOT! Be courageous and kind, praying for the person (Matthew 5:44), and looking up to God for support. Before long, you will overcome evil with good (Romans 12:21), and be on the next level of your accomplishment.

Chapter 11
Generosity

We have been given different gifts to manage, and God requires we share these gifts. As someone who is living in dominion, you are blessed. And everyone who is blessed is blessed to be a blessing unto others. In Deuteronomy 12:6, we are given different channels through which we can exercise our generosity. It says, "And there you shall bring your burnt offerings and your sacrifices, your tithes and the offering that you present, your votive offerings, your freewill offerings, and the firstlings of your herd and of your flock." So, you have to be generous through giving of alms (donations), making offerings at Mass/Church service and tithing.

Give Alms

Prayer is efficacious when accompanied by fasting, almsgiving, and righteousness. A small amount given with righteousness is better than much with wrong doing: "It is better to give alms than to treasure up gold. For almsgiving delivers from death, and it will purge away every sin. Those who perform deeds of charity and of righteousness will have fullness of life; but those who commit sin are the enemies of their own life" (Tobit 12:8-10). Almsgiving here is not giving because I have received from someone else or because I am going to get a tax receipt, but giving because I have been blessed by God and in a position to help a brother or a sister who is in need. When we give only to those who gave to us, we are not doing anything different from the pagans, the tax collectors, the Gentiles and the hypocrites (Matthew 5:46). This kind of giving is what Kevin Stirratt in his book, "A Generous Life", referred to as "Back Scratching" where one gives because one hopes to get something in return.

We have to model our almsgiving and donations after the giving of Christ who gave without counting the cost and without expecting any "tax receipt" in return: "If I am to be like Jesus, I am to generously pour my life into others as an act of unbridled grace. I am not to take up the mentality of a back-scratcher, which is "I'll give when I'm given to, and in equal measure." (Stirratt, 2012) When you take a closer look at the text above, you cannot help but wonder if it is really possible to give outside the mentality of back-scratching. The Bible says "Give, and it will be given to you…" (Luke 6:38). The point being made here is: When you give, don't expect a pay back or favour in return from the direct recipient. Let your hope for reward be in God. In other words, if there must be any back-scratching, let it be from the Lord.

In your charitable donations and giving, expect God alone to be your "back scratcher". That is the kind of spirit that should govern the giving of one who is living in dominion. The scripture says, "He who is kind to the poor lends to the Lord, and he will repay him for his deed" (Proverbs 19:17). Jesus buttressed this point in his conversation with the man who had invited him for a dinner. He said to him, "When you give a dinner or a banquet, do not invite your friends or your brothers or your kinsmen or rich neighbours, lest they also invite you in return, and you be repaid. But when you give a feast, invite the poor, the maimed, the lame, the blind, and you will be blessed, because they cannot repay you. You will be repaid at the resurrection of the just" (Luke 14:12-14).

What is Jesus saying in essence? We all know that it is not a feasible thing to have a feast or celebration without the company of friends, brothers, sisters and other relatives. Jesus is only saying that we should not be exclusive in our invitation because God's kingdom is open to everyone. Our generosity and kindness should cut across class and race to all and sundry. More so, we are not to expect a reward from them, for our rich reward is in God!

Make Good Offering

St. Paul was clear in his teaching on giving/offering when he said, "The point is this: the one who sows sparingly will also reap sparingly, and the one who sows bountifully will also reap bountifully. Each of you must give as you have made up your mind, not reluctantly or under compulsion, for God loves a cheerful giver. And God is able to provide you with every blessing in abundance, so that by always having enough of everything, you may share abundantly in every good work" (2 Corinthians 9:6-8). Every blessing that we have comes from God. Our money and material possessions are all given to us by God. These do not result from your smartness but by the grace of God. It is clear from the scriptures, that you have been abundantly blessed to the point that you have enough of everything. And it goes on to say that "you may share abundantly in every good work". The good work ranges from supporting the Church and its projects to ensuring that structures for justice and peace are well maintained and financed.

For Christians, this has to also do with your weekly or daily offerings in the Church: Are they proportionate to the blessings that the Lord has given to you? As someone living in dominion, you must make it a point of duty to always make a bountiful offering to the Lord. This kind of offering is given cheerfully as a sign of thanksgiving in gratitude for all that you have received from the Lord. It is important to note that, God is interested in our giving because it is an indication of where our heart is. If your heart is with God, you will want to give to a cause that will advance His kingdom on earth. As such, your offerings will be made not out of duty or obligation, but from a cheerful heart. That is the kind of offering that is pleasing to God.

The scripture says, "You shall season all your cereal offerings with salt; you shall not let the salt of the covenant with your God be lacking from your cereal offering; with all your offerings, you shall offer salt" (Leviticus 2:13). In ancient Middle Eastern lands, an agreement was sealed with a gift of salt to show the strength and permanence of the contract. Salt also points to the effects of a truthful agreement. For us today, the best salt with which we can make our offering is – A CHEERFUL HEART! A heart that is full of appreciation and devoid of hatred, grudges and malice.

Hence, Jesus says, "If you are offering your gift at the altar, and there remember that your brother has something against you, leave your gift there before the altar; first be reconciled to your brother, and then come and offer your gift" (Matthew 5:23). Thus, reconciliation is the needed salt. We all know what salt does to food; makes it tasty, and can also be used for preservation. Making sure that our hearts are free of every grudge and are cheerful does the same thing to our offering. A cheerful and loving heart is the required seal over our offerings. So as one living in dominion, you must ensure this seal in your offerings. Otherwise, you will be sowing in an arid ground.

Tithe

A tithe is one tenth of annual produce or earnings, contributed or given in support of the Church and clergy. It has its origin in biblical time. In the scriptures, God commanded "Bring the full tithe into the storehouse, that there may be food in my house; and thereby put me to the test, says the Lord of hosts; if I will not open the windows of heaven for you and pour down for you an overflowing blessing (Malachi 3:10).

And in Leviticus 27:30, he says, "All the tithes of the land, whether of the seed of the land or of the fruit of the trees, is the Lord's; it is holy to the Lord". In other words, tithe is a divine portion and should not be tampered with. For us today, it translates into one tenth of our salary or 1/10 of everything you receive as a student, newly settled apprentice, worker (employer/ employee), and even as a house wife. One can choose to give it monthly or annually. You are free in this regard. But the percentage has already been decided and fixed by the Lord.

Talking about Divine Portion, Genesis 2:9.17 comes to mind: "And out of the ground the Lord God made every tree grow that is pleasant to the sight and good for food. The tree of life was also in the midst of the garden, and the tree of the knowledge of good and evil... but of the tree of the knowledge of good and evil you shall not eat, for in the day that you eat of it you shall surely die." God is saying, "I will never curse you, but if you eat of this tree, you will curse yourself. Your discipline over this one tree is how you show your love to me." Compare that to the injunction of the Lord on tithe; "You are cursed with a curse, for you are robbing me; the whole nation of you" (Malachi 3:9). That is God's Word concerning those who don't bring their tithe to the storehouse. And you can see some similarity with the Genesis experience. It's the same thing that God said about tithe: If you eat or consume the tithe you are cursed with a curse. God is not in the business of cursing his people, but you can curse yourself by your behaviour of spending your tithe which you shouldn't have spent since it is a divine portion meant for the up keep of the Church.

The devil will want to talk you into not contributing/ giving your tithe just the way he talked Adam and Eve into eating the tree at the middle of the garden. He knows that the day they eat the divine portion, they have to leave the place, and he needs the place. The enemy may deceive you to spend your tithe, to violate the divine portion because he needs your job, position or finances. So, beware!

There are three things you must know about tithe:

1. Through it we acknowledge that everything comes from God. It is not your boss or the company you work for that has blessed you. They may have served as the channel, but God is the one who has blessed you. The earth and its fullness belong to God. … (Psalm 24). "The silver is mine, and the gold is mine", says the Lord of host (Haggai 2:8). So, God controls all the wealth of the world (Matthew

28:18), and has power over your work. This is the more reason why you should partner with him.

2.   Through it we bring our finances under God's protection. In Malachi 3:11, the scripture says, "I will rebuke the locust for you, so that it will not destroy the produce of your soil; and your vine in the field shall not be barren, says the Lord of hosts."

3.   Through it we cast down any struggle we have to worship the gift over the giver. Particularly as one's income goes up it becomes more important and more difficult. The love of money, the Bible says, is the root of all evil. Not the money itself. God blessed the children of Israel with the wealth of Egypt. It was they who turned it into an idol. God gave them the gold; they turned the gold into an idol. You can easily turn your income into an idol. And as you grow up, one of the ways you keep yourself from trusting in your resources is to bring your tithe. When you bring your tithe, you cast down every idol: you are saying – GOD YOU CAN TRUST ME TO BLESS ME AGAIN BECAUSE NO MATTER HOW HIGH I GET, I WILL PUT YOU FIRST!

Part 3
Refueling the Dominion Life

As one who lives in dominion, there is always the need for recreation and reflection; for the replenishment of lost strength and renewal of spirit and zeal. You need to constantly refuel yourself. In this last part of the book, I will be discussing certain practices that will help you not only to build your spiritual and physical/social stamina, but will also aid you in gaging it when it begins to run low.

Chapter 12
Retreat and Vacation

"The apostles returned to Jesus and told him all that they had done and taught. And he said to them, "Come away by yourselves to a lonely place, and rest a while." For many were coming and going, and they had no leisure even to eat. And they went away in the boat to a lonely place by themselves. Now many saw them going, and knew them, and they ran there on foot from all the towns, and got there ahead of them. As he landed he saw a great throng, and he had compassion on them, because they were like sheep without a shepherd; and he began to teach them many things" (Mark 6:30-34).

The disciples were extremely tired. They had gone forth for the Lord and carried out his mission, and it had exhausted them. In spite of that, the crowds were still pressing on them so much so that they had little or no time to make their reports, rest and meditate. Thus, Jesus suggested they go to a quiet place and be alone with God for a while. In other words, to work effectively one needs periodic rest and renewal. When I see people bragging that they have worked for five or ten years without vacation, I just lower my head. Then, from my heart comes this feeling of pity and strong concern that expresses, "Oh, how I wish you understand what you are doing to yourself." Retreat and vacation are not luxurious activities. They are necessities that will help you to take time out and replenish some lost strength, physically or spiritually.

I love the above biblical text so much, especially when I am exhausted. One must face the fact that your profession, work or ministry saps energy. Both physical and mental power is drained from you on a daily basis as you go back and forth in your endeavour trying to make ends meet. As such, from time to time, there is need for a relief from this work pressure. At intervals, just take off and get some rest. From experience, you will come back rejuvenated, ready to work with renewed strength, zeal and vigour with better ideas and clearer vision. Above all, your working relationship with co-workers (colleagues, subordinates, boss, etc.), will improve. You will no longer transfer aggression and backbite, which you did as a result of stress and work pressure in the office. Since you would have rested well and have your head cleared up. This will create an atmosphere where you feel in charge. Not just of your work, but also of your emotions and work relationships. And that is what it means to live in dominion.

In like manner, the spirit of man from time to time needs some extended periods alone with God in meditation, study and prayer. This is where retreat becomes very necessary. You need to constantly make quality time to listen to God speak to you about your life as a whole and what His plans are for you concerning your family, work and future prospects. The scripture says, "To him the gatekeeper opens; the sheep hear his voice, and he calls his own sheep by name and leads them out. When he has brought out all his own, he goes before them, and the sheep follow him, for they know his voice" (John 10:3-4). One way of knowing the voice of God is to constantly commune with him in your quiet time. Retreat creates this atmosphere of silence and helps one to recollect and listen to the voice of God in nature. As prophesied by Isaiah, your ears shall hear a word behind you saying, "This is the way, walk in it" (Isaiah 30:21).

When I was made a chaplain for the Catholic Men Organisation (CMO) of Our Lady of Fatima Cathedral Kano in 2007, which was shortly after my ordination to the priesthood, I did not know where to start from. As such, I resented the office. I dwelled upon a number of negative feelings and thoughts: Why the CMO? A group that is struggling to survive? During their prayer meetings you find only 3 persons at the beginning, and on a good day, they may be up to 6 or 7 at the time the meeting is coming to an end. Look at me a newly ordained priest, do they want to kill me? Okay, why didn't they make me a chaplain to the youth? They are looking for someone to kill. In fact, I am not going to do anything. These were the questions and thoughts that were going on in my head for more than six months, and I was unable to accomplish a thing in this group. I couldn't make any impact with such negative thoughts and defeated spirit. But lo and behold, during my first personal retreat as a priest, (I had made a resolution after my ordination, to go on personal retreat every other year), my attitude toward this group was completely and divinely transformed.

The retreat lasted a whole week. On the third day, in the course of my meditation, God brought the group up as an issue to be pondered upon. When God played the tape for me, and I pictured the group in my mind and what my attitude to the group has been, I was humbled. In the spirit of remorse for running away from my responsibility all the while, and avoiding what God was calling me to do, acknowledging my pride and arrogance, I prayed and asked God for mercy, insight and direction on the way to go. On the fourth day during meditation, ideas began to flood my mind on what to do, and those ideas when we put them into practice, gave birth to the "NEW FACE OF CMO" with over 200 men registering on the 1st day.

This is just one fruit or result of a retreat. I have got a number of such after eleven years as a priest. So when you retreat, your life will not only have a divine direction, it will be fruitful and divinely sustained in dominion.

Chapter 13
Physical Exercise

"If you give these instructions to believers, you will be a good servant of Christ Jesus, as you feed yourself spiritually on the words of faith and of the true teaching which you have followed. But keep away from those godless legends, which are not worth telling. Keep yourself in training for a godly life. Physical exercise has some value, but spiritual exercise is valuable in every way, because it promises life both for the present and for the future. This is a true saying, to be completely accepted and believed." 1 Timothy 4:6-9 (GNB)

Keep yourself in training for a godly life. Physical Exercise has some value, but spiritual exercise is valuable in every way... It is interesting to see how sometimes one tries to say one thing, but ends up saying two. Or one says one thing, and the listener grabs two. Just like the Psalmist said, "Once God has spoken; twice have I heard this: that power belongs to God" (Psalm 62:11). St Paul's focus in the above passage is on godliness, but at the same time highlights the importance of exercise for physical fitness. Some people marvel when they see me at the gym, and some in the Church walk up to me and ask "Father, do you work out?" When I answer "Yes!" the expression on their faces is like – what kind of priest goes to the gym? And I always answer their unspoken question in my heart – "The priest that knows 1 Timothy 4:8."

Physical exercise is generally considered as health a health enhancing activity, which as St Paul says, is valuable because it helps one to reduce the risk of developing diseases such as cardiovascular disease, type 2 diabetes, mellitus, osteoporosis, and obesity, and some forms of cancer, like colorectal and breast cancer (Kohl 2001; Kriska 2003; World Health Organization 2002). So, physical exercise is necessary for fitness, good health, weight loss, and good looks, etc. More so, research has shown that those who exercised the equivalent of 30-35 miles running/walking a week face half the risk of premature death compared to those who exercised equivalent of five miles or less per week (Morrison & Bennett, 2012). In other words, the more one partakes in physical exercise, the better it is for one. Physical exercise can be a planned activity like taking a walk, going swimming or to the gym regularly at a stipulated time. It can also be physical activity generated by body movement as one goes about one's daily activity like shopping, walking to school/work instead of driving, or even walking the dog. However, it is important to intentionally schedule physical exercises with a sense of purpose.

According to Morrison and Bennett (2012), "Regular exercise, particularly low-impact exercise or weight-bearing exercise such as walking and dancing, is not just important to bone development in the young but is also important to the maintenance of peak levels of bone density during adulthood" (P.95). Besides the physical benefits, there are also psychological and spiritual benefits. Psychologically, physical exercise elevates one's mood and decreases the risk of anxiety, depression, and low self-esteem (Lox, Martin Ginis & Petruzzello, 2006). These psychological benefits have been attributed to various biological mechanisms like (a) the release of the body's own natural opiates into the blood stream, which produce a 'natural high' and act as a painkiller, (b) stimulation of the release of catecholamines such as noradrenaline and adrenaline, which counter any stress response and enhance mood, and (c) muscle relaxation, which reduces feelings of tension (Morrison & Bennett, 2012: pp. 96).

Spiritually, physical exercise enables one to stay longer in prayers and transcendental meditation and even helps one to study longer. I have observed that after physical exercise, I can study intensely for four hours without getting tired. Physical exercise builds strength in one and gives one the right disposition to work, study or pray.

So for one called to live in dominion, the importance of physical exercise cannot be over emphasised. To be in charge, you must be in good health - physically, psychologically, spiritually, and otherwise. And you need to live out your days on earth as ordained by the Lord. It is within your reach not to allow disease to cut short your God-given life due to lack of exercise and bad diet. Hence, physical exercise is an activity that one should indulge in joyfully without compulsion. Make a schedule and be committed to it joyfully.

Having said that it is also important to note that extremes are to be avoided. As Aristotle opined, "Virtue lies in the middle". It doesn't make sense when you allow the missing of your exercise to cause you guilt feelings. Or allowing yourself to be carried away by excessive exercise to the detriment of time with family. It has been observed that the long-term physical consequences of excessive exercising relate to muscle wastage and weight loss rather than to any specific disease (Morrison & Bennett, 2012). The point here is moderation!

There are different recommendations for exercise; some recommend 30 minutes of moderate intensity exercise on at least 5 days of each week for adults. And for children, 60 minutes daily of at least moderate intensity exercise is recommended (Department of Health, 2004; cited in Morrison & Bennett, 2012).

Personally, I've been keeping to at least 60 minutes' workout three or four time a week; depending on how busy the week gets. And this has been awesome for me. So, it's all about moderation and what works for you. But be sincere about it and don't get lazy. Otherwise, you will be found wanting in the area of physical health, and that would diminish your God-given gift – to be in charge, (all aspects of dominion). Don't forget – Health is Wealth!

Chapter 14
Knowledge of Sources of Support

Even youths shall faint and be weary, and young men shall fall exhausted; but they who wait for the Lord shall renew their strength, they shall mount up with wings like eagles, they shall run and not be weary, they shall walk and not faint (Isaiah 40: 30-31).

As human beings, we are limited. There is a level to which our strength can carry us. Once we begin to exceed this limit, we get tired, exhausted, burned-out, and stressed. Sometimes the feeling of emptiness sets in, we get angry unnecessarily, and nothing interests us. We are fagged out by work and the weariness of life. We have our house chores staring at us, but we lack the strength to do them. Our study table become messy, and our closet in disarrayed, but we are too weak to arrange them or put them in order. In other times too, it is the troubles of life; a loved one has just die, or you have just had a fight with a friend, or a broken relationship, or lost a job. The list can go on and on. In such moments, we find ourselves at our wit ends. That is the exact time that we need to look out for our sources of support.

Delay in such circumstance can be dangerous. Don't allow it to linger on for too long without crying out for help. A number of persons who delayed in calling out for support, or stretching out their hands for the embrace of a friend at a time like this, ended up with depression or committed suicide. Worst of all, it may be a problem with your belief system, which if not arrested on time can lead to loss of faith. It is important to note that every human person needs spiritual and social support.

1. Spiritual Support

This is more than just belonging to a faith group. It goes beyond the practice of a religious belief. Belonging to a religious body and practicing a religious belief could be a means of getting spiritual support but it is not all of it. For real spiritual support, you need to have a spiritual mentor (like a spiritual director) or small group, with whom you consult on the matters of faith and spiritual life. The scripture is clear on this when it says, "Iron sharpens iron, and one man sharpens another" (Proverbs 27:17). When iron blades are robbed together, each becomes sharper and thus more effective. Likewise, when believers are involved in one another's lives, mutual edification takes place.

According to Hemrick (2010), When we are under extreme pressure a sense of the sacred reminds us that God is ultimately in charge of our life" (p. 5). One of the objectives of spiritual support is to purify the lens with which you are looking at your concerns, problems, challenges or current situation. It helps you to see things for what they really are in the light of Christ (Mark 4:22; Luke 8:17; Ephesians 5:11-14). Otherwise, you will be left with only the world's lens. And when pressure or trouble is seen through the eyes of the world alone, they become necessary, meaningless evils. But when they are envisioned through the eyes of God, they are seen as purposeful (since God allowed them), and encourage us to pursue that purpose: "Searching for and seeing God's purpose is our best means for depleting the pressures we feel" (Hemrick, 2010: p. 5).

One of the best ways to search and seek out God's purpose for your life, or to figure out the way to go in each tight and confusing situation is to avail yourself of good spiritual direction. Spiritual direction takes a closer and deeper look into our relationship with the spiritual aspect of being human. This is also what a spiritual support group can do for you, which is like what Spiritual Care providers do for patients in the hospital.

In the Western world, especially in US and Canada, Spiritual Caregiving is available in hospitals and care home. Whereby a spiritual care provider visits patients in the hospital or senior residents in their home to know how they are faring. In most cases, both the care-giver and the care receiver end up having an awesome experience. The Story below titled "I'VE GOT NO FRIEND", is a true life experience of one of my classmates in my first Unit of Clinical and Pastoral Education (CPE). He shared it as one of his Critical Learning Experiences.

I've Got No Friend!!

On this cold winter morning, having finished my initial visits, I decided to wander around the ward to see if there is anyone I could chat up. Most of the patients had visitors by their bedside and I decided not to disturb this family time. However, down the hall was Jimmy sitting by himself on the bed and watching the television. I decided to visit with Jimmy and say hello. Jimmy turned away from the television and returned by greeting. I reminded him that I had visited him the week before and just dropped by to see how he was doing. When he said he was fine, I asked if he had had friends or family visiting him recently. Immediately I said this, his countenance changed and he looked at me sternly before saying, "I got no friends".

I was touched not just by Jimmy's words but also by the way he said them and the look in his eyes. Connecting Jimmy's words with the experience of other patients who were receiving visitors, I sensed Jimmy's feelings to be a mixture of anger and annoyance. As such, I moved closer to him to inquire why he would say he had no friends. When he was not forthcoming with any response, I made him realize that I was his friend and that was why I had come to visit with him. As I was saying this, a lady who plays the guitar for patients on the 7th floor came to his bed side and began to sing. I joined in the singing and we sang many songs for Jimmy starting from Dolly Patton's "Coat of Many Colours". As if the lady heard my discussion with Jimmy before she came in, she later began to sing, "Lean on me, when you're not strong, I'll be your friend ..." At that point, Jimmy began to cry. I asked him if anything was wrong but he said "these are tears of joy!" Consequently, I told him that now he's got not just me as his friend but also the guitar lady! The smiles on Jimmy's face lighted up the room!

The above magic or transformation was made possible as a result of the spiritual support that was provided by my classmate (the spiritual caregiver). Otherwise, Jimmy would have remained in his gloomy state, which can also lead to other complications in his health or process of recovery. As Dr Vivian Walker opined, "Life could be painful on other levels other than physical." And study has shown that spiritual and emotional traumas sometimes play themselves out as physical pains. When not handled from the root, the patient may end up taking pain killers that will only rub the surface, as the pain never goes away completely. You can only get to the root of such pains through spiritual support.

So, who are you relying on for spiritual support? From whom do you request prayers when you find it difficult and hard to pray for yourself and family? Who do you normally talk to when you have something bothering your conscience, or when you are grappling with an article of faith? If you don't have anyone for these spiritually related issues, then, it is high time you got one. As a priest, there have been times when parish, family and personal problems weighed seriously on me, and all I could remember doing was calling another priest friend or a number of lay friends with whom I share my spiritual journey to talk with them and also ask them to assist me with their prayers. Other times too, I just book an appointment with my Spiritual Director and go see him for some discussion. This has proven to be very helpful to me in such moments, and I believe that it can help you too.

The Spiritual Director must be someone you can trust or confide in. Someone you can freely open up to, and who is capable of giving you a spiritually informed counsel. It can be a priest, a pastor or reverend in the Church, or a respected member of your Church. It can also be a small faith group of about 2-5 people in which you come together to pray and share your spiritual struggles and challenges. Any of these can serve, the problem is not having one. And when you don't have such support, the devil can easily defeat you when you are weak or going through faith crisis. As one called to live in spiritual dominion, you constantly need the support of a spiritual director or of a spiritual support group.

2. Social Support

What do you do when you are emotionally low? Who do you talk to when you are angry, sad or mad?

I remember seeing a picture of a little boy walking all alone in a beautiful isolated highway with the caption, "Sometimes it is better to be alone no one can hurt you." When I showed it to a friend, he said, "But you can hurt yourself". There are times in life that we prefer or choose to go solo on the path of life like the boy on the picture. But like my friend said; what are the chances that you might not hurt yourself? If something is bothering you, that needs to be shared with a close friend, and you bottle it up for too long, that can be dangerous. Moreover, when one anger is bottled up upon another, and another upon another, it gets to a point when it can no longer be contained. The end result will be explosion. This can manifest itself in different ways; it could bring about both mental and physical illness. This is one of the reasons we need friends with whom we can talk and share our feelings.

It was Thomas Hughes who said, "Blessed are they who have the gift of making friends, for it is one of God's best gifts. It involves many things, but above all, the power of going out of one's self, and appreciating whatever is noble and loving in another." This saying by Hughes, reminds me of the conclusion of my classmate when he presented Jimmy's story. He said, "The kind of friendship I established with Jimmy this day did not come about just as I walked into the room but it took some effort of planting myself by his bedside and the instrumentality of the guitar lady who coincidentally sang a music which conveyed the message I was trying to pass across to Jimmy." Friendships sometimes just happens, but at other times, we have to make effort. One thing is sure; it's worth the effort when you find a true friend. A true friend will joyfully sing with you when you are on the mountain top, and silently walk beside you in the valley.

In Ecclesiastes 4: 9-12, the scripture says, "Two are better than one, because they have a good reward for their toil. For if they fall, one will lift up his fellow. But woe to him who is alone when he falls and has not another to lift him up! Again, if two lie together, they keep warm, but how can one keep warm alone? And though a man might prevail against one who is alone, two will withstand him – a threefold cord is not quickly broken." As human beings we are created to be relational and to fellowship with one another (Genesis 2:18). When we are living in a healthy relationship or fellowship, we rely on one another and help one another. David and Jonathan relied on one another, and supported each other (1 Samuel 18:1-5; 20:1-17); Mary, Martha, and Lazarus supported Jesus Christ (Luke 10:38-42), and Jesus Christ equally supported them in return (John 11:17-37). In our social and work/academic life, we need to support one another.

Do you have a colleague of yours that you can easily run to at work when you have a difficult task in front of you? Maybe for some ideas, clarification or enlightenment. As a student, is there any of your classmates whom you can easily approach whenever you find it difficult to understand a subject or a particular topic? At least for some further simplified explanation and discussion. These are important sources of support that we all need in our lives as relational beings. No one is an island. Some shy away from this kind of support due to pride. Remember the scriptures; "Pride goes before destruction, and a haughty spirit before a fall" (Proverbs 16:18); "Whoever exalts himself will be humbled, and whoever humbles himself will be exalted" (Matthew 23:12). Come to think of it, even if it is from a little child that you got an idea, when you will put it to use, the child won't be there to say, "Hey, I taught him that!" People will only marvel at your ability and knowledge and compliment you, or give praise and glory to God.

As people called to live in dominion, it is important for us to know our sources of support; who to go to when we are in need. Jesus was clear about his sources of support: When he needed spiritual support, he went away to a quiet place to converse with the Father (Luke 5:16), when he felt like socializing, he looks for Mary and Martha, and their brother Lazarus. When invited to a dinner or called for a pastoral duty, and he needed a side kick to go with him, he looked out for Peter, James and John (Mark 5:21-43; Luke 8:40-56), or just one of the three. Hence, the need for us to choose our friends wisely. In making friends, look out for people who take responsibility for their own lives and circumstances. They are generally those with good lives and good character. They are the friends you want. When you have the type of friends who blame others – God, the economy, the government, their childhood, etc., once they run out of things to blame, they will pick you! So, look closely at how friends talk and think and make sure they tend to have a responsible worldview.

You will hardly get all the support that you need from one person. Social support can further be broken down into emotional, moral, financial, work and academic supports. So don't mix them up. If you are lucky, you may get two or three from one person. But you have to be super lucky to get all five in one person. It is very rare. Honour each of those relationships and see them as valuable. Don't compare one to the other, they are different sources of support, helping you meet different human needs.

3. Spiritual Care for the Sick

There is no mention in the scripture of anytime that Jesus was sick. But lots of times, the sick were either brought to him, or reported to him for healing (Matthew 12:22). The fact that he was able to heal the sick is a sign of his dominion over sickness. He showed his dominion over demons by casting them out and silencing them or making them mute (Mark 1:21-34). Likewise, we saw his dominion over nature when he calmed the storm of the sea (Mark 4:35-41).

The scripture says that one of the signs that shall follow us as Christians is that we shall pray for the sick and they will recover (Mark 16:18). If you have faith as little as the mustard seed, you will say to this mountain, move from here to there; and it will move (Matthew 17:20-21). You will say to the mulberry tree be uprooted and be planted… and they will obey you. This the dominion we have and share in Jesus Christ.

As human beings, sometimes we get sick. We get sick not because we have sinned, or because we are weak, but as a result of the wearing and tearing of our body tissues. We wear ourselves out with overtime at work and lack of rest. Sometimes too, sickness comes as a result of an accident or taking in a poisoned food or something that you are allergic to. No doubt, at other times, we fall sick due to carelessness. But whatever the cause of the sickness, the point I am trying to make is that sickness is part of our human existence and experience. It is not something to be ashamed of or to hide. If it comes, it comes... and you need all the available resources that can help you tackle it. As someone called to live in dominion, who has the tendency of becoming sick, you should be aware of the sources of support available to you whenever you are sick. During sickness, you will need some support; either from family, friends, or community of faith. This is where the role of Spiritual Care for the sick becomes very significant in our hospitals.

Spiritual Caregivers are trained professionals who give care and support to the sick in the hospitals, hospices, and care homes. They are trained in a way that they can give spiritual care and support to patients or residents irrespective of their religious background, faith denominations and spiritual practices. They are interested in whatever concern care-receivers, which in a way could be aggravating their current situation of ill health or old age. Studies have shown that emotional/spiritual worries sometimes manifest as physical pain (Puchalski, 2006). The medical practitioners, in such cases, may end up handling only the effect of the problem without being able to get to the root cause of the problem, sickness or pain. This is where Spiritual Care becomes necessary.

From my experience and those of my colleagues in Spiritual Care giving, I also see Spiritual Caregivers as those who come in when the family or friends of the sick are either far away or not there. So, it is important to ask the hospital management if they have such services when you are sick, on admission in the hospital, and need this kind of support. Besides the gift of presence that they bring to you, they also help you to see things from another lens and can also pray with you or for you if you are open to it. No doubt, sometimes when we are sick, it is difficult to pray. But you can also ask them to pray with you or for you. Knowing this, is essential to one called to live in dominion. So that when the need arises, you can easily tap into this knowledge. Knowing what support you need at a given time and where and how to get it, is power in itself.

4. Mentoring

When you hear the word mentor or mentoring, what comes to your mind? For some people it is a business term, or a word use in motivation psychology. While for some others it is just another English word. One of the teachers in the Oxford School of Coaching & Mentoring, Eric Parsloe (2016), defined mentoring as supporting and encouraging people to manage their own learning in order for them to maximize their potential, develop their skills, improve their performance and become the person they want to be (as cited in MentorSET, 2016). Going by this definition, mentoring is a powerful tool that can help us develop and grow in every aspect of our life. A good spiritual mentor can help you grow in your spiritual life. A good mentor in your field of work, business or study can help you achieve your goal. So, in mentoring, there is a mentor and one that is being mentored. That is, the mentee.

A mentor is a guide, who has a very good grasp and better knowledge of the direction that a mentee wants to go or of the goal that the mentee wants to achieve. Most often, the mentor has tread the same path in the past. Hence, he brings to this new relationship (the mentor and the mentee relationship), a wealth of experience. Therefore, a good mentor is empathetic and understanding, because he has been through it and knows the challenges that the mentee is facing or going through. People who are living in dominion are expected to be good mentors and mentees. The mentors help the mentees to learn how to live in dominion, and also live in dominion, themselves.

A good example of a mentor and a mentee relationship in the Scripture is that between Paul and Timothy. Timothy was brought up, as a child, in a Christian home. He is a good example of someone who was influenced by godly relatives. His mother, Eunice, and grandmother, Lois, were Jewish believers who helped shaped his life and promote his spiritual growth (2 Timothy 1:5; 3:15). But in answering his call as a leader in the Church, he was schooled under Paul. Hence, Bible scholars refer to him as Paul's protégé; a young person who is taught and helped by someone who has a lot of experience.

This is well captured in 'Paul's Charge to Timothy': "Now you have observed my teaching, my conduct, my aim in life, my faith, my patience, my love, my steadfastness, my persecution, my sufferings, what befall me at Antioch, at Ico'nium, at Lystra, what persecution I endured; yet from them all the Lord rescued me. Indeed, all who desire to live a godly life in Christ Jesus will be persecuted, while evil men and impostors will go on from bad to worse, deceivers and deceived. But as for you, continue in what you have learned and have firmly believed, knowing from whom you learned it and how from childhood you have been acquainted with the Sacred Writings which are able to instruct you for salvation through faith in Christ Jesus" (2 Timothy 3:10-15). In Paul's own words, it is evident that he mentored Timothy.

In another instance, addressing the Corinthians Paul said, "I do not write this to make you ashamed, but to admonish you as my beloved children. For though you have countless guide in Christ, you do not have many fathers. For I became your father in Christ Jesus through the gospel" (1 Corinthians 4-15). Here Paul acknowledges the existence of mentors. He said, "For though you have countless guide in Christ", those are mentors. People who are helping others to understand and practice the faith. When addressing some of the issues that the Church in Corinth raised with regards to what is lawful and what is not; what meat is clean and edible and which is not, Paul gave a beautiful answer: "All things are lawful," but not all things are helpful. "All things are lawful," but not all things build up. And he concluded that discuss by saying boldly, "Be imitators of me, as I am of Christ" (1 Corinthians 10:23 – 11:1). That is the voice of a good mentor. A good mentor will challenge you to watch how he does things or handles tasks. So that you can learn and be able to handle them yourself or do them on your own, and possibly graduate to also become a mentor to your younger ones.

You cannot remain a mentee all your life. A time comes when a mentee becomes a mentor too. Though from time to time one can still fall back to one's mentor for advice. Timothy graduated from being a mentee and Paul invested a lot of confidence in him. He sent him on errands and believed that he was going to represent him well. When he sent him to the Corinthians, he said to them, "I urge you then, be imitators of me. Therefore I sent to you Timothy, my beloved and faithful child in the Lord, to remind you of my ways in Christ, as I teach them everywhere in every Church" (1 Corinthians 4:16-17). Though Timothy was already on his own, as a Church leader, Paul never stopped encouraging and advising him. Paul advised Timothy on such practical topics as qualifications for Church leaders, public worship, confronting false teaching, and how to treat various groups of people within the Church.

It is appropriate to engage a mentor, whenever you find yourself in a new career, a new vocation, a new field of study, a new environment, etc. You need a guide; you need someone who not only has the map of where you are going, but who also knows how to read the map because he has been there. As a newly ordained priest, you need a mentor; as someone just finally professed as a religious, you need a mentor; as a newly married man or woman you need a mentor. In this case, someone who has accumulated years in your new field. You need a godly mentor – living out the call in an exemplary way. The relationship should be a helpful one based upon mutual trust and respect that will help you live out your Christian calling or vocation. If that person is not helping you to live out your Christian vocation well, as you should, then, he or she is not a mentor. This is especially the case because a mentor is a guide who can help the mentee to find the right direction and who can help him or her to develop solutions to career and vocational issues. A mentor can also be one of your sources of support as one called to live in dominion.

Chapter 15
Summary

We have a God who loves us so much, and who believes in us as his own children. As such, he has given us dominion (power and responsibility) over everything he created, not for absolute domination, but for nurture and care. As Pope **Francis** aptly puts it, if we read the biblical texts in their context, with an appropriate hermeneutic, we shall understand that the dominion given to us by God requires that we "till and keep" the garden of the world. God wants us to be in loving charge of all other created things, and not them being in-charge of us. God wants us to be happy and supportive of each other. He wants to see us living and enjoying life to the full. This is the reason he came to earth and took flesh (John 10:10), and it is for the same reason that we are called to live in dominion. Jesus wants us to be physically, psychologically, socially and spiritually alive and active through consciousness of who we are in him. We are to live each day acknowledging and appreciating God's gift in our life and being mindful of his promises as we live out these principles of obedience, holiness, hard work, prayer, divine wisdom, courage and generosity.

References

Adelaja, S. (2015). Accessing Divine Wisdom. Retrieved from http://www.godembassy.com/main/pastor-sunday-adelaja/item/746-accessing-divine-wisdom.html

Ann, V. (2010). One thousand gifts: A dare to live fully right where you are. Zondervan, Grand Rapids, Michigan 49530

Catholic Conference of Catholic Bishops (1992). Catechism of the Catholic Church. Publications Service, 90 Parent Avenue, Ottawa (Ontario) K1N 7B1

Coutinho, P. (2009). Just as you are: Opening your life to the infinite love of God. Chicago: Loyola Press.

Flannery, A. (Ed). (2007). Vatican Council II: The basic sixteen documents. New York: Costello Publishing Company.

Hemrick, E. (2010). Combating Pressure with Joy: A Priest's Perspective. Human Development (31), 1, 25 – 29. Retrieved from http://www.eds.a.ebscohost.com.ezproxy.liv.ac.uk/eds/pdfviewer/pdfviewer

Kelly, M. (2010). Rediscover Catholicism: A spiritual guide to living with passion and purpose. Beacon Publishing.

Kohl, H. W. (2001). Physical activity and cardiovascular disease: evidence for a dose-response. Medicine and Science in Sports and Exercise, 33: S472-S487.

Kriska, A. (2003). Can a physically active lifestyle prevent type 2 diabetes? Exercise and Sports Science Review, 31: 132 - !37.

Lox, C. L., Martin Ginis, K. A. and Petruzzello, S. J. (2006). The Psychology of Exercise: Integrating Theory and Practice (2nd Ed). Scottsdale, AZ: Holcomb Hathway.

McGregor, J. (2013). Only 13 Percent of People Worldwide Actually like Going to Work. Retrieved from http://www.washingtonpost. com/news/on-leadership/wp/2013/10/10/only-13-percent-of-people-worldwide-actually-like-going-to-work/?utm_term=,502c983e98c2

MentorSET (2016). What is Mentoring? Retrieved from http://www.mentorset.org.uk/what is mentoring.html

Morrison, V., & Bennett, P. (2012). An introduction to health Psychology (3rd Ed). Pearson Education Limited, Edinburg Gate Harlow. Essex CM202JE, England.

Nouwen, H., J., M. (1986). Reaching Out: The Three Movements of the Spiritual Life. Doubleday, a division of Bantam Doubleday Dell Publishing Group, Inc. 1540 Broadway, New York, New York 10036

Puchalski, C., M. (2006). A time for listening and caring: Spirituality and the care of the chronically ill and dying. Oxford University Press, Inc. 198 Madison Avenue, New York 100016.

Rolheiser, R. (2014). Sacred fire: A vision for a deeper human and Christian maturity. New York: Image Crown Publishing Group, a division of Random House LLC, a Penguin Random House Company.

Ryan, L. (2016). The Top Ten Reasons People Hate their Jobs. Retrieved from http://www.fastsupport.com

Stirratt, K. (2012). A Generous Life. Beacon Hill Press, Kansas City.

The National Mentoring Partnership (2017). The Mentoring Effect. Retrieved from http://www.mentoring.org/program-resources/mentor-resources-andpublications/the-mentoring-effect/?gclid

World Health Organization (2002). The World Health Report: Reducing Risks, Promoting Healthy Life. Copenhagen: WHO Regional Office for Europe.

Printed in Canada